NICE URDŪ TEACHER

Fully English Transliterated With Hindi help

उर्दू के फराटेदार माहिर बनाने वाली किताब ।

اردو کے فراٹے دار ماہر بنانے والی کتاب

This book will make you learn Urdu from grounds up.

by

Prof. Ratnakar Narale

RatnakaR

PUSTAK BHARATI
BOOKS-INDIA

Author :

Dr. Ratnakar Narale, *Ph.D. (IIT), Ph.D. (Kalidas Sanskrit Univ.);*

Prof. Hindi, Ryerson University, Toronto
web : www.books-india.com * email : books.india.books@gmail.com

Book Title : Nice Urdu Teacher
Nice Urdu Teacher is a unique work founded on serious R&D. With Field Tests it was concluded that a Urdu Book must clearly and comparatively demonstrate the Four Distinct Positions of each of the 39 Urdu Characters, in order to be a successful Urdu Teacher. Therefore, the first 39 chapters, along with their comparative charts, of this book are intelligently devoted for this vital aspect.

It is a step-by-step systematic approach with cumulative learning from the basic alphabet to making your own Urdu sentences comfortably. It walks you carefully holding your finger. It is fully English transliterated for your help. It is also coupled with Devanagari script for those who understand India's National Language Hindi. It has nice diagrams, colourful Chart of Alphabet, valuable Tables, Answers to all Exercises and Examples, Transliterated Students' Dictionary of vocabulary, important Notes at the beginning of each chapter and at each step, and much more. It is second to none! It is so nice, that the crooks are pirating it under fake print and e-publications.

Fonts used in the Book :

Ratnakar-u for Nastā'leeq typing

Publisher and Distributor :
PUSTAK BHARATI (Books-India)
Division of PC Plus Ltd.,
email : books.india.books@gmail.com web : www.books-india.com

ISBN 978-1-897416-35-8
90000
9 781897 416358

ISBN 978-1-897416-35-8

INDEX

Urdū Chart of Alphabet, Nastā'leeq (Indo-Persian) Script — Back Cover

Front Cover Design : — Ratnakar Narale

Lesson 1 The Urdu Alphabet — 7

Lesson 2 The Urdu Accent Marks *(nuqte नुक्ते)* — 15

Lesson 3 Joining Urdu Letters : — 16

LESSON TITLE	: SUBJECT	LESSON	PAGE
Joining Urdū letter	The 39 Urdū Characters	3.0	10
	A. The Urdū Character Properties		11
	B. The Udrū Character Shapes		14
	C. The Urdū Character Connectors		16

UDRU LETTERS GROUP 1

The 1st letter of the Urdū Alphabet : *alif* अलिफ़ ا (**English** *a* **हिंदी अ**)	3.1	25
The 2nd letter of the Urdū Alphabet : *be* बे ب (**English** *b* **हिंदी ब**)	3.2	27
The 3rd letter of the Urdū Alphabet : *pe* पे پ (**English** *p* **हिंदी प**)	3.3	28
The 4th letter of the Urdū Alphabet : *te* ते ت (**English** *t* **हिंदी त**)	3.4	30
The 5th letter of the Urdū Alphabet : *ṭe* टे ٹ (**English** *ṭ* **हिंदी ट**)	3.5	32
The 6th letter of the Urdū Alphabet : *se* से ث (**English** *s* **हिंदी स**)	3.6	33

UDRU LETTERS GROUP 2

The 7th letter of the Urdū Alphabet : *jīm* जीम ج (***English*** *j* **हिंदी ज**)	3.7	35
The 8th letter of the Urdū Alphabet : *che* चे چ (**English** *ch* **हिंदी च**)	3.8	37
The 9th letter of the Urdū Alphabet : *baḍī he* बड़ी हे ح (**English** *h* **हिंदी ह**)	3.9	38
The 10th letter of the Urdū Alphabet : *khe* ख़े خ (**English** *kh* **हिंदी ख़**)	3.10	40

UDRU LETTERS GROUP 3

The 11th letter of the Urdū Alphabet : *dāl* दाल د (**English** *d* **हिंदी द**) 3.11 41

The 12th letter of the Urdū Alphabet : *ḍāl* डाल ڈ (**English** *ḍ* **हिंदी ड**) 3.12 43

The 13th letter of the Urdū Alphabet : *zāl* ज़ाल ذ (**English** *z* **हिंदी ज़**) 3.13 45

The 14th letter of the Urdū Alphabet : *re* रे ر (**English** *r* **हिंदी र**) 3.14 46

The 15th letter of the Urdū Alphabet : *aḍe* अड़े ڑ (**English** *ḍ* **हिंदी ड़**) 3.15 48

The 16th letter of the Urdū Alphabet : *zay* ज़े ز (**English** jh, z **हिंदी झ, ज़**) 3.16 49

The 17th letter of the Urdū Alphabet : *zhe* ज़े ژ (**English** z **हिंदी ज़्य**) 3.17 51

UDRU LETTERS GROUP 4

The 18th letter of the Urdū Alphabet : *sīn* सीन س (**English** *s* **हिंदी स**) 3.18 53

The 19th letter of the Urdū Alphabet : *shīn* शीन ش (**English** *sh* **हिंदी श**) 3.19 54

The 20th letter of the Urdū Alphabet : *suād* सुआद ص (**English** *s* **हिंदी स**) 3.20 56

The 21st letter of the Urdū Alphabet : *jhuād* ज़ुआद ض (**English** *j* **हिंदी ज**) 3.21 58

UDRU LETTERS GROUP 5

The 22nd letter of the Urdū Alphabet : *toe* तोए ط (**English** *t* **हिंदी त**) 3.22 60

The 23rd letter of the Urdū Alphabet : *zoe* ज़ोए ظ (**English** *jh* **हिंदी ज़**) 3.23 62

The 24th letter of the Urdū Alphabet : *ain* ऐन ع (**English** *e* **हिंदी ए**) 3.24 64

The 25th letter of the Urdū Alphabet : *gain* ग़ैन غ (**English** *gh* **हिंदी ग़**) 3.25 65

The 26th letter of the Urdū Alphabet : *fe* फ़े ف (**English** *f* **हिंदी फ़**) 3.26 67

The 27th letter of the Urdū Alphabet : *qāf* क़ाफ़ ق (**English** q **Hindi क़**) 3.27 68

UDRU LETTERS GROUP 6

The 28th letter of the Urdū Alphabet : *kāf* काफ़ ک **(English *k* Hindi क)**	3.28	70
The 29th letter of the Urdū Alphabet : *gāf* गाफ़ گ **(English *g* Hindi ग)**	3.29	72
The 30th letter of the Urdū Alphabet : *lām* लाम ل **(English *l* Hindi ल)**	3.30	73
The 31st letter of the Urdū Alphabet : *mīm* मीम م **(English *m* Hindi म)**	3.31	75
The 32nd letter of the Urdū Alphabet : *nūn* नून ن **(English *n* Hindi न)**	3.32	76

UDRU LETTERS GROUP 7

The 33rd letter of the Urdū Alphabet : *vāo* वाओ و **(Eng. *v, w* Hindi व, उ)**	3.33	78
The 34th letter of the Urdū Alphabet : *chhoṭī he* छोटी हे ہ **(Eng. *h* Hindi ह)**	3.34	80
The 35th Urdu letter : *do chashmī he* दो चश्मी हे ھ **(English *h* Hindi ह)**	3.35	82
Urdu Breath Characters हुरूफ़ मुरक्कब حروف مرکب		84
The 36th letter of the Urdū Alphabet *hamzā* हमज़ा ء **(English *i* Hindi इ)**	3.36	85
The 37th Urdu letter : *chhoṭī ye* छोटी ये ی **(English *y* Hindi य, इ)**	3.37	86
The 38th Urdū alphabet : *baḍī ye* बड़ी ये ے **(English *e* Hindi ए)**	3.38	88
The 39th Urdū alphabet : *nūnegunnaḥ* नूनगुन्न: ں **(English *an* Hindi ँ)**	3.39	90
Study of multiple letter words دو سے سات تک حرفوں والے لفظوں کے جملوں کی مشق	3.40	91

Lesson 4	**Writing Hindi and English Vowels in Urdu**	95
Lesson 5	Urdu Diacritical Accent Marks	98
Lesson 6	The Urdu Numerals	104
Lesson 7	Making your own urdu sentences, **Present, Past, Future**	111
Lesson 8	**Making Sentences for Completed Actions**	129
Lesson 9	**Ratnakar's Brain Surgery of Urdu Grammar**	135
Lesson 10	**Use of the Case Suffixes (post-positions)**	137
Lesson 11	Adjectives and Adverbs	149
Lesson 12	General Knowledge and Vocabulary	155
Lesson 13	**Urdu Conversational Road map**	175
Lesson 14	Urdu Literature	183

LESSON 1

THE URDU ALPHABET

उर्दू हुरूफ़ तहज्जी, उर्दू वर्ण माला *urdū hurūf tahajjī* اردو حروف تہجی

The Urdu alphabet has 39 characters. Following chart shows their alphabetical order and their 'Stand-alone' shapes. When the Urdu letters are not Stand alone, but joined 'to other letters, they may be written differently, as shown in the following lessons

No.	उर्दू नाम	Urdū name	Hindī ihḍI equivalent	English equivalent	Nastālīq نستعلیق نویس script
.	**अलिफ़**	***alif***	अ	a	ا
2.	**बे**	***be***	ब	b	ب
3.	**पे**	***pe***	प	p	پ
4.	**ते**	***te***	त	t	ت
5.	**टे**	***ṭe***	ट	ṭ	ٹ
6.	**से**	***se***	स	s	ث
7.	**जीम**	***jīm***	ज	j	ج
8.	**चे**	***che***	च	ch	چ

9.	बड़ी हे	*badi he*	ह	h	ح
10.	ख़े	*khe*	ख़	kh	خ
11.	दाल	*dāl*	द	d	د
12.	डाल	*ḍāl*	ड	ḍ	ڈ
13.	ज़ाल	*zāl*	ज़	j	ذ
14.	रे	*re*	र	r	ر
15.	अड़े	*aḍe*	ड़	ḍ	ڑ
16.	ज़े	*zay*	ज़	jh, z	ز
17.	ज़े (ज़्ये)	*zhe*	ज़	z	ژ
18.	सीन	*sīn*	स	s	س

19.	शीन	***shīn***	श	sh	ش
20.	सुआद	***suād***	स	s	ص
21.	ज़ुआद	***zuād***	ज़	jh	ض
22.	तोए	***toe***	त	t	ط
23.	ज़ोए	***zoe***	ज़	jh	ظ
24.	ऐन	***ain***	ए, अ	e, a	ع
25.	ग़ैन	***ghain***	घ	gh	غ
26.	फ़े	***fe***	फ़	f	ف
27.	क़ाफ़	***qāf***	क़	q	ق
28.	काफ़	***kāf***	क	k	ک
29.	गाफ़	***gāf***	ग	g	گ
30.	लाम	***lām***	ल	l	ل
31.	मीम	***mīm***	म	m	م
32.	नून	***nūn***	न	n	ن

33.	वाओ	*vāo*	व	v	و
34.	छोटी हे	*chhoṭī he*	ह	h	ہ
35.	दो चश्मी हे	*do chashmī he*	ह	h	ھ
36.	हमज़ा	*hamzā*	इ	i	ء
37.	छोटी ये	*chhoṭī ye*	य	y	ی
38.	बड़ी ये	*baḍī ye*	ए	e	ے
39.	नूनगुन्ना	*nūngunnā*	अँ	an	ں

NOTE : Please remember the resembling sounds in Urdu

ت	ط			ق	ک		خ
ث	س	ص	س		ی	ے	
ج		ز	ژ	ض	ظ		
ح	ہ	ھ		و		ڈ	

EXERCISE *mashq* (مشق मश्क) 1 : **Letters at random** बे तरतीब हुरूफ़। بےترتیب حروف

Recognize the Urdū letters scattered at rondom.

ف		ک	ھ	چ	
د		ع		ٹ	
	ن		پ		ھ
	ف	ہ		ڈ	
	خ		ص		ے
		ب		گ	
	ج		ش		ی
ث		م		ط	
ض		ژ		ا	
	و		ح	ت	ء
ز		س		ل	

THIS EXERCISE IS IMPORTANT. PLEASE DO NOT GO TO LESSON 2, WITHOUT DOING THIS PROPERLY.

THE URDU NASTALIQ ALPHABET
उर्दू- नस्तलीक़ वर्ण माला * उर्दू नस्तलीक़ हुरूफ़ तहज्जी
1 अलिफ़ a
2 बे b
3 पे p
4 ते t
5 टे ṭ
6 से s
7 जीम j
8 चे ch
9 बड़ी हे h
10 ख़े kh
11 दाल d
12 डाल ḍ
13 ज़ाल j
14 रे r
15 अड़े ḍ
16 ज़े z
17 झ़े zh
18 सीन s
19 शीन sh
20 सुआद s
21 जुआद xj
22 तोए t
23 ज़ोए j
24 ऐन e
25 ग़ैन gh
26 फ़े f
27 क़ाफ़ q
28 काफ़ k
29 गाफ़ g
30 लाम l
31 मीम m
32 नून n
33 वाओ v
34 छोटी हे h
35 दो चश्मी हे h
36 हमज़ा h
37 छोटी ये y
38 बड़ी ये y
INDEX
Urdu Character Number
Urdu Name
English
Urdu Character
i.stand alone
ii. at starting position
iii. at middle position
iv. at the end position
AMIR KHUSRAV
BAHADUR SHAH ZAFAR
MIRZA GHALIB
KAIFI AZMI
FIRAQ GORAKHPURI
MUHAMMAD RAFI
ISBN 978-1-897416-08-2
The Urdu Learning Book
0 siphar
1 ek
2 do
3 tīn
4 chār
5 pāñch
6 chhah
7 sāt
8 ātha
9 nau

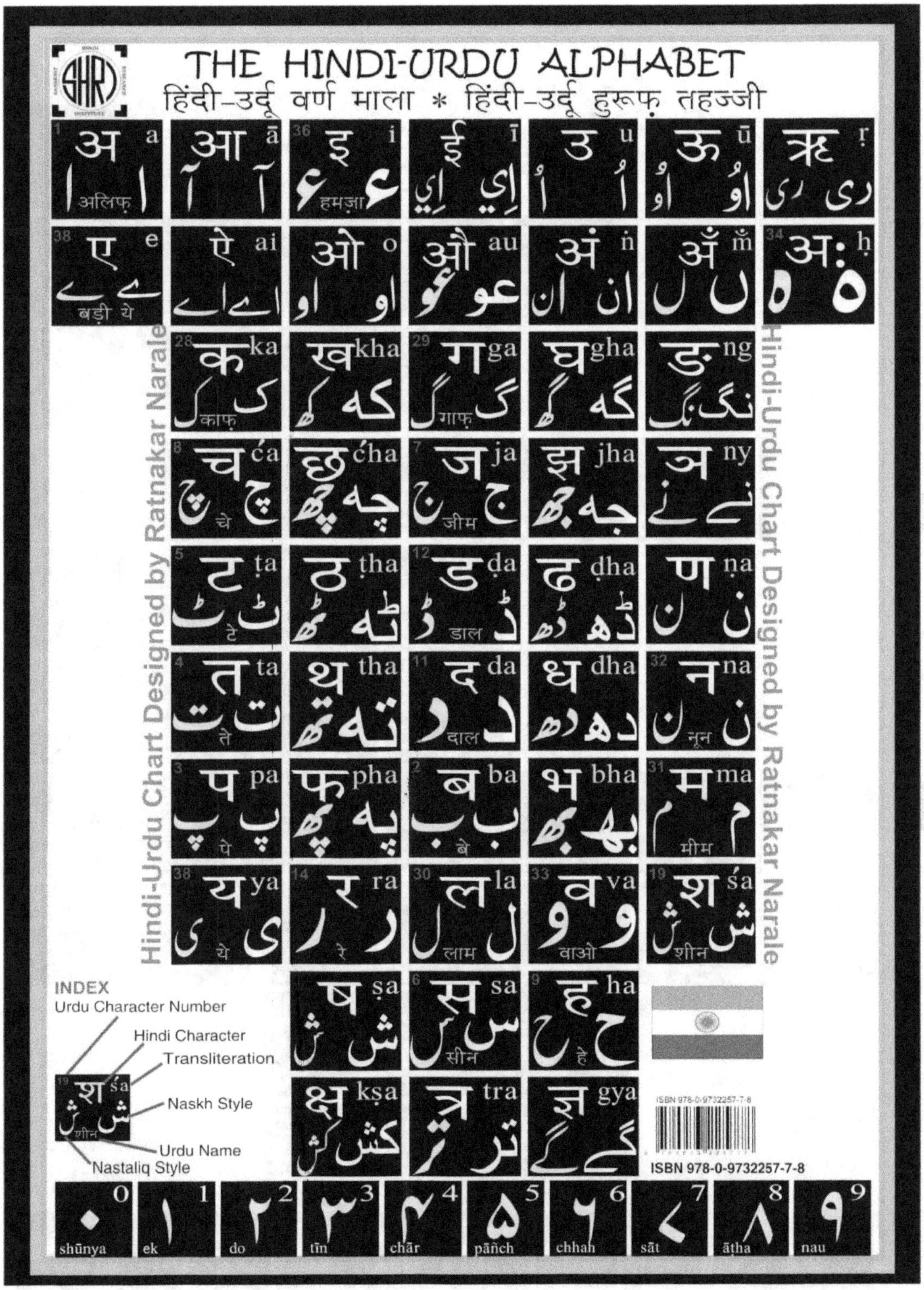
THE HINDI-URDU ALPHABET
हिंदी-उर्दू वर्ण माला * हिंदी-उर्दू हुरूफ़ तहज्जी
अ a अलिफ़
आ ā
इ i हमज़ा
ई ī
उ u
ऊ ū
ऋ ṛ
ए e बड़ी ये
ऐ ai
ओ o
औ au
अं ṅ
अँ m̐
अः ḥ
क ka काफ़
ख kha
ग ga गाफ़
घ gha
ङ ng
च ća चे
छ ćha
ज ja जीम
झ jha
ञ ny
ट ṭa टे
ठ ṭha
ड ḍa डाल
ढ ḍha
ण ṇa
त ta ते
थ tha
द da दाल
ध dha
न na नून
प pa पे
फ pha
ब ba बे
भ bha
म ma मीम
य ya ये
र ra रे
ल la लाम
व va वाओ
श śa शीन
ष ṣa
स sa सीन
ह ha हे
क्ष kṣa
त्र tra
ज्ञ gya
Hindi-Urdu Chart Designed by Ratnakar Narale
INDEX
Urdu Character Number
Hindi Character
Transliteration
Naskh Style
Urdu Name
Nastaliq Style
ISBN 978-0-9732257-7-8
0 shūnya
1 ek
2 do
3 tīn
4 chār
5 pāñch
6 chhah
7 sāt
8 āṭha
9 nau

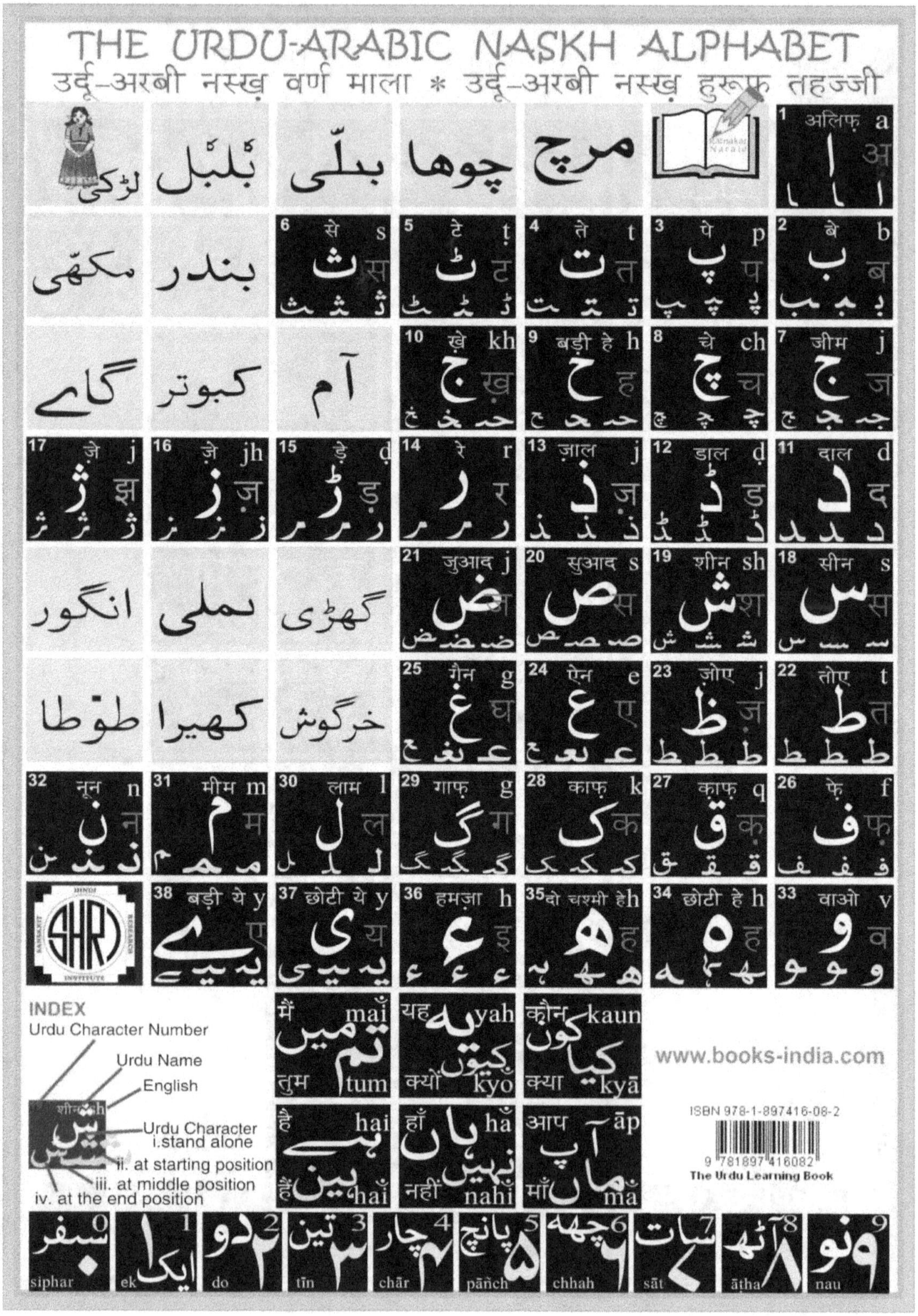

THE URDU-ARABIC NASKH ALPHABET
उर्दू-अरबी नस्ख़ वर्ण माला * उर्दू-अरबी नस्ख़ हुरूफ़ तहज्जी
INDEX
Urdu Character Number
Urdu Name
English
Urdu Character
i.stand alone
ii. at starting position
iii. at middle position
iv. at the end position
www.books-india.com
ISBN 978-1-897416-08-2
The Urdu Learning Book
siphar
ek
do
tīn
chār
pāñch
chhah
sāt
ātha
nau

LESSON 2

THE DOTS / MARKS

नुक़्ते *nuqte* نقطے

In Urdū many letters are recognized simply by looking at the dots (marks) attached to them. Following are the letters which can be identified with dots and similar looking non-dot letters.

			ث	ٹ	ت	پ	ب
ا				چ	ج	خ	ح
م					ذ	ڈ	د
ہ				ژ	ز	ڑ	ر
ء			ض	ص		ش	س
ی			غ	ع		ظ	ط
ے			گ	ک		ق	ف
					ں	ن	ل

EXERCISE *mashq* (مشق मश्क) **2 :** The dots (marks) नुक़्ते *nuqte* نقطے

Write each of the above letters and remove or add the dots to see how it changes.

PLEASE DO NOT GO TO LESSON 3, WITHOUT DOING PREVIOUS LESSON PROPERLY.

LESSON 3

Ratnakar's General Rules for the Following Chapters

JOINING THE URDU LETTERS

हर्फ़ों का जोड़ना। حرفوں کا جوڑنا

THIS IS THE MOST CRITICAL **BUT INTERESTING AS WELL AS UNIQUE ASPECT in learning urdu language. It is important for English and Hindi knowing people to understand how the letters are truncated or symbolized when two, three or more letters are joined. I hope you have learned previous lessons well and you are able to read individual Urdu letters easily, if not, please go back to lesson 1.**

LESSON 3.0

THE 39 URDU CHARACTERS

The 39 Urdu Characters

suād	shīn	sīn	zhe	zay	aḍe	re	zāl	ḍāl	dāl	khe	he	che	jīm	se	ṭe	te	pe	be	alif
ص	س	س	ر	ر	ر	ر	د	د	د	ح	ح	ح	ح	ٮ	ٮ	ٮ	ٮ	ٮ	ا
Table Designed by Ratnakar Narale.																			
nun gunna		ye	ye	hamza	he	he	vāo	nūn	mīm	lām	gāf	kāf	quāf	fe	ghain	ain	zoe	toe	juād
ں		ے	ی	ء	ھ	ہ	و	ں	م	ل	گ	ک	ق	ف	ع	ع	ط	ط	ص

PITFALLS :

In order to understand Urdu clearly and easily, consideration of the following Three things (ppp) is essential. (A) Character Properties; (B) Character Positions and (C) the Connector Points.

In Hindi and to a certain extent in English, what you right is what you read. In Urdu it is different. In Urdu the Stand Alone characters change their shapes when they are joined. **This is the crux of learning to read/write Urdu. You will notice that, when a character with any dots/mark comes between two other characters, only its dots/mark is written. This representation of a character only by its dots/mark is called** Shosha **शोशा شوشہ . This makes Urdu language very fascinating for a learner.**

(A) THE CHARACTER PROPERTIES

Unique for a Language born in India, most of the Urdu characters can be recognized simply by looking at the 'placement, number and presence or absence' of the

dots/dots or a mark (नुक्ता *nuqtā* نقطہ) in them. Some say there are 37 characters in

Urdu language, other people say there are 38 characters, I say there are 39 characters. These 39 characters can be grouped into sets, according to their above mentioned three properties.

(a) According to their 'shapes,' the Urdu lettere may be grouped into the following four sets.

i. 1, 2 or 3 dots : غ ظ ض ش ژ ز ذ خ چ ج ث ٹ ت پ ب ں ق ف (ی=) یٖ

ii. No dots : ل ک ع ط س ر د ح ا ی ء ھ ہ و م ے

iii. Presence of ط shape : ڈ ڑ

iv. Presence of a line : گ

(b) Again, unique for a Language originated from Sanskrit (Sanskrit's grand-daughter, Hindi's daughter), Urdu is not only written Right to Left, but Nastā'leeq words can be stacked and compacted, vertically and/or diagonally. Thus best suited for caligraphy. e.g.

فج (*faj* फ़ज, Mountain pass), جہنم (*jahannam* जहन्नम, Hell), خنجر (*khanjar* खंजर, Daggar),

گھر (*ghar* घर, House) حنفی (*haneefee* हनीफ़ी, Sect)

بچپن (*bachpan* बचपन, Childhood), کسی سے (*kisee se* किसी से, To someone),

محمد (Muhammad मुहम्मद) بطخ (*battakh* बत्तख़, Duck),

پیچھے (पीछे, Behind), نیچے (नीचे, Below), بیچ (बीच, Between), سر (सिर, Head)

(B) THE CHARACTER SHAPES

Also, unique for the Languages of India, Urdu characters are written in four different shapes, depending up on their position in a word. See below :

(1) STAND ALONE POSITION : When a single letter is written as a stand-alone character, it is written in complete shape, along with its dot (नुक़्ता *nuqtahā* نقطہ), if any. e.g. see the 39 Stand-alone Urdu characters, as identified above.

(2) STARTING POSITION : When there are two or more letters in a word, the first letter is written in "Starting Position.' the last letter in its End position and the rest in their Middle positions.

For example : सब *sab* (all) سب (*sīn* س is written in Starting shape, and *be* ب in End shape); सबक़ *sabaq* (Lesson) سبق (*sīn* س is written in Starting shape, *be* ب in Middle and *qāf* ق in End position)

NOTE : Urdu words can start from 37 of the 39 characters. Their Starting shapes are :

Urdu Characters in STARTING POSITION

Side-by-side Comparison

The 39 Urdu STAND ALONE Characters :

suād	shīn	sīn	zhe	zay	aḍe	re	zāl	ḍāl	dāl	khe	he	che	jīm	se	ṭe	te	pe	be	alif
ص	س	س	ر	ر	ر	ر	د	د	د	ح	ح	ح	ح	ٮ	ٮ	ٮ	ٮ	ٮ	ا
Table Designed by Ratnakar Narale.																			
nun gunna		ye	ye	hamza	he	he	vāo	nūn	mīm	lām	gāf	kāf	quāf	fe	ghain	ain	zoe	toe	juād
ں		ے	ی	ء	ھ	ہ	و	ں	م	ل	گ	ک	ق	ف	ع	ع	ط	ط	ص

The 37 Urdu Characters at STARTING Position :

suād	shīn	sīn	zhe	zay	aḍe	re	zāl	ḍāl	dāl	khe	he	che	jīm	se	ṭe	te	pe	be	alif
صـ	شـ	سـ	ژ	ذ		ر	ذ	ڈ	د	خـ	حـ	چـ	جـ	ثـ	ٹـ	تـ	پـ	بـ	ا
Table Designed by Ratnakar Narale.																			
nun gunna		ye	ye	hamza	he	he	vāo	nūn	mīm	lām	gāf	kāf	quāf	fe	ghain	ain	zoe	toe	juād
		ے	یـ	عـ	ھـ	ہـ	و	نـ	مـ	لـ	گـ	کـ	قـ	فـ	غـ	عـ	ظ	ط	ضـ

NOTE : (1) ade ڑ never comes in Starting position. (2) Nun-gunna ں never comes in Starting position.

TIP 1 : The letters such as अलिफ़ *alif* (ا), दाल *dāl* (د), डाल *ḍāl* (ڈ), ज़ाल *jāl* (ذ); रे *re* (ر), अड़े *aḍe,* (ڑ), ज़े *zay* (ز), ज्ये *zhe* (ژ) and वाओ *vāo* (و), NEVER connect with the next letter on their LEFT side.

TIP 2 : When a letter that DOES NOT connect on its LEFT side (see Tip 1), comes in the begining of a word, it is written in Stand alone position. e.g. rab रब رب

TIP 3 : Anywhere in a word, when a letter DOES NOT connect on its LEFT side (see Tip 1), but comes after another letter that also DOES NOT connect on its Left side, both are written in their Stand alone positions. e.g. aur और اور

(3) MIDDLE POSITION : When there are three or more letters in a word,

(i) the first letter is written in Starting Position.

(ii) the last letter in End position,

(iii) The rest are in Middle position, as shown below. 38 of the 39 characters can come

in the middle of a word.

When the Middle letters connect with the letter on their Right side, their shapes are :

Urdu Characters in MIDDLE POSITION

Side by side Comparison

The 39 Urdu STAND ALONE Alone Characters :

suād	shīn	sīn	zhe	zay	ṛe	re	zāl	ḍāl	dāl	khe	he	che	jīm	se	ṭe	te	pe	be	alif
ص	س	س	ر	ر	ر	ر	د	د	د	ح	ح	ح	ح	ٮ	ٮ	ٮ	ٮ	ٮ	ا
Table Designed by Ratnakar Narale.																			
nun gunna	ye	ye	hamza	he	he	vāo	nūn	mīm	lām	gāf	kāf	quāf	fe	ghain	ain	zoe	toe	juād	
ں	ے	ی	ء	ھ	ہ	و	ں	م	ل	گ	ک	ق	ف	ع	ع	ط	ط	ص	

The 38 Urdu Characters at MIDDLE Position :

suād	shīn	sīn	zhe	zay	ṛe	re	zāl	ḍāl	dāl	khe	he	che	jīm	se	ṭe	te	pe	be	alif
ـصـ	ـشـ	ـسـ	ـژ	ـز	ـڑ	ـر	ـذ	ـڈ	ـد	ـخـ	ـحـ	ـچـ	ـجـ	ـثـ	ـٹـ	ـتـ	ـپـ	ـبـ	ـا
Table Designed by Ratnakar Narale.																			
nun gunna	ye	ye	hamza	he	he	vāo	nūn	mīm	lām	gāf	kāf	quāf	fe	ghain	ain	zoe	toe	juā d	
	ـے	ـیـ	ـئـ	ـھـ	ـہـ	ـو	ـنـ	ـمـ	ـلـ	ـگـ	ـکـ	ـقـ	ـفـ	ـغـ	ـعـ	ـظـ	ـطـ	ـضـ	

NOTE : Nun gunna ں never comes in Middle position.

TIP 4 : **The letters that DO NOT connect on their LEFT side (see Tip 1 above), are written SAME in their Middle position as they are in their End position. e.g. (i) *jā* जा جا (ii) *jān* जान جاں**

(4) END POSITION : When there are two or more letters in a word, **(i) the first letter is written in "Starting Position.' (ii) the last letter in End Position and (iii) the rest (if any) are in Middle Position.**

For example : सबक् *sabaq* (Lesson) سبق (*sīm* س is written in Starting shape, *be* ـبـ is written in 'Middle shape' and *qāf* ق is in End shape).

All 39 characters shown above can come at the End of a word. **When the End letters connect with the letter on their Right side, their shapes are :**

Urdu Characters in END POSITION

Side-by-side Comparison

The 39 Urdu STAND ALONE Alone Characters

suād	shīn	sīn	zhe	zay	aḍe	re	zāl	ḍāl	dāl	khe	he	che	jīm	se	ṭe	te	pe	be	alif
ص	س	س	ر	ر	ر	ر	د	د	د	ح	ح	ح	ح	ٮ	ٮ	ٮ	ٮ	ٮ	ا
Table Designed by Ratnakar Narale.																			
nun gunna		ye	ye	hamza	he	he	vāo	nūn	mīm	lām	gāf	kāf	quāf	fe	ghain	ain	zoe	toe	juād
ں		ے	ی	ء	ھ	ہ	و	ں	م	ل	گ	ک	ق	ف	ع	ع	ط	ط	ص

The 39 Urdu Characters at END Position

suād	shīn	sīn	zhe	zay	aḍe	re	zāl	ḍāl	dāl	khe	he	che	jīm	se	ṭe	te	pe	be	alif
ـص	ـش	ـس	ـژ	ـز	ـڑ	ـر	ـذ	ـڈ	ـد	ـخ	ـح	ـچ	ـج	ـث	ـٹ	ـت	ـپ	ـب	ـا
Table Designed by Ratnakar Narale.																			
nun gunna		ye	ye	hamza	he	he	vāo	nūn	mīm	lām	gāf	kāf	quāf	fe	ghain	ain	zoe	toe	juād
ں		ـے	ـی	ـء	ـھ	ـہ	ـو	ـن	ـم	ـل	ـگ	ـک	ـق	ـف	ـغ	ـع	ـظ	ـط	ـض

TIP 5 : **If the End letter comes after a letter that DOES NOT connect on its LEFT side (see Tip 1), the End letter is written in it's Stand alone position. e.g. urdū उर्दू اردو**

TIP 6 : **Following is the summary of above discussion :**

(a) Character shapes that are same in Middle and End position :

The Middle position and the End position is same for the characters that do not connect on their left side (see Tip 1),

(b) Character shapes that are same in End and Stand alone position :

As an End character, when ANY of the 39 characters appears AFTER अलिफ़ *alif* (ا),

character दाल *dāl* (د), डाल *ḍāl* (ڈ), ज़ाल *jāl* (ذ); रे *re* (ر), अड़े *aḍe*, (ڑ), ज़े *zay* (ز),

ज्ये *zhe* (ژ) or वाओ *vāo* (و), the *alif* (ا) is written in Stand alone shape.

(C) THE URDU CHARACTER CONNECTORS

Again, uncommon for the Languages born in india, the connected ends of Urdu letters are truncated into joining points or suitable handles in order to make smooth connections with the characters that comes on its Left and/or Right side, respectively.

(1) STARTING POSITION :

As said above, the left half portion of the characters, other than those characters which do not connect on their left side (see Tip1), is cut off into a Flat Connector Point, so that the next character on left side butts and connects with it smoothly.

Connector Points in STARTING POSITION

Side-by-side Comparison

The 39 Urdu STAND ALONE Alone Characters

suād	shīn	sīn	zhe	zay	aḍe	re	zāl	ḍāl	dāl	khe	he	che	jīm	se	ṭe	te	pe	be	alif
ص	س	س	ر	ر	ر	ر	د	د	د	ح	ح	ح	ح	ب	ب	ب	ب	ب	ا
Table Designed by Ratnakar Narale.																			
nun gunna	ye	ye	hamza	he	he	vāo	nūn	mīm	lām	gāf	kāf	quāf	fe	ghain	ain	zoe	toe	juād	
ں	ے	ی	ء	ھ	ہ	و	ں	م	ل	گ	ک	ق	ف	ع	ع	ط	ط	ص	

The 28 Urdu Characters at STARTING Position

suād	shīn	sīn	zhe	zay	aḍe	re	zāl	ḍāl	dāl	khe	he	che	jīm	se	ṭe	te	pe	be	alif
صـ	شـ	سـ								خـ	حـ	چـ	جـ	ثـ	ٹـ	تـ	پـ	بـ	
Table Designed by Ratnakar Narale.																			
nun gunna		ye	ye	hamza	he	he	vāo	nūn	mīm	lām	gāf	kāf	quāf	fe	ghain	ain	zoe	toe	juād
			يـ	ئـ	ھـ	ہـ		نـ	مـ	لـ	گـ	کـ	قـ	فـ	غـ	عـ	ظـ	طـ	ضـ

NOTE : The ELEVEN Urdu Letters, अलिफ़ *alif* (ا), दाल *dāl* (د), डाल *ḍāl* (ڈ), ज़ाल *zāl* (ذ); रे *re* (ر), अड़े *aḍe*, (ڑ), ज़े *zay* (ز), ज्ये *zhe* (ژ) and वाओ *vāo* (و), बड़ी ये *badī ye* (ے) and नून गुन्ना *nūn gunnā* (ں)

DO NOT connect with the next letter on their LEFT side, therefore they do not need connector handles.

(2) MIDDLE POSITION : The characters which do not connect on left side (see Tip 1) have only connector point on right side.

The Connector Points in MIDDLE POSITION

Side by side Comparison

The 39 Urdu STAND ALONE Alone Characters

suād	shīn	sīn	zhe	zay	aḍe	re	zāl	ḍāl	dāl	khe	he	che	jīm	se	ṭe	te	pe	be	alif
ص	ں	ں	ر	ر	ر	ر	د	د	د	ح	ح	ح	ح	ٮ	ٮ	ٮ	ٮ	ٮ	ا
Table Designed by Ratnakar Narale.																			
nun gunna		ye	ye	hamza	he	he	vāo	nūn	mīm	lām	gāf	kāf	quāf	fe	ghain	ain	zoe	toe	juād
ں		ے	ی	ء	ھ	ہ	و	ں	م	ل	گ	ک	ق	ف	ع	ع	ط	ط	ص

The 38 Urdu Connectore Points in MIDDLE Position

suād	shīn	sīn	zhe	zay	aḍe	re	zāl	ḍāl	dāl	khe	he	che	jīm	se	ṭe	te	pe	be	alif
ـصـ	ـشـ	ـسـ	ـژ	ـز	ـڑ	ـر	ـذ	ـڈ	ـد	ـخـ	ـحـ	ـچـ	ـجـ	ـثـ	ـٹـ	ـتـ	ـپـ	ـبـ	ـا

Table Designed by Ratnakar Narale.																		
nun gunna	ye	ye	hamza	he	he	vāo	nūn	mīm	lām	gāf	kāf	quāf	fe	ghain	ain	zoe	toe	juād
	ـے	ـیـ	ـئـ	ـھـ	ـہـ	ـو	ـنـ	ـمـ	ـلـ	ـگـ	ـکـ	ـقـ	ـفـ	ـغـ	ـعـ	ـظـ	ـطـ	ـضـ

NOTE : नूने गुन्ना *nūn gunnā* (ں) DOES NOT come in Middle Position.

(3) END POSITION : In End position, the characters in full shape are attached a 'Connector handle' on their right side, to provide a connector point for the letter on right side. (*hamzā* and *nūn-gunnā* are exceptions, as they do not connect on right).

Connector Points in END POSITION

Side by side Comparison

39 Urdu STAND ALONE Alone Characters

suād	shīn	sīn	zhe	zay	aḍe	re	zāl	ḍāl	dāl	khe	he	che	jīm	se	ṭe	te	pe	be	alif
ص	س	س	ر	ر	ر	ر	د	د	د	ح	ح	ح	ح	ٮ	ٮ	ٮ	ٮ	ٮ	ا
Table Designed by Ratnakar Narale.																			
nun gunna		ye	ye	hamza	he	he	vāo	nūn	mīm	lām	gāf	kāf	quāf	fe	ghain	ain	zoe	toe	juād
ں		ے	ی	ء	ھ	ه	و	ں	م	ل	گ	ک	ق	ڡ	ع	ع	ط	ط	ص

39 Urdu Connectore Points in END Position

suād	shīn	sīn	zhe	zay	aḍe	re	zāl	ḍāl	dāl	khe	he	che	jīm	se	ṭe	te	pe	be	alif
ـص	ـش	ـس	ـژ	ـز	ـڑ	ـر	ـذ	ـڈ	ـد	ـخ	ـح	ـچ	ـج	ـث	ـٹ	ـت	ـپ	ـب	ـا
Table Designed by Ratnakar Narale.																			
nun gunna		ye	ye	hamza	he	he	vāo	nūn	mīm	lām	gāf	kāf	quāf	fe	ghain	ain	zoe	toe	juād
ں		ـے	ـی	ـء	ـھ	ـہ	ـو	ـن	ـم	ـل	ـگ	ـک	ـق	ـف	ـغ	ـع	ـظ	ـط	ـض

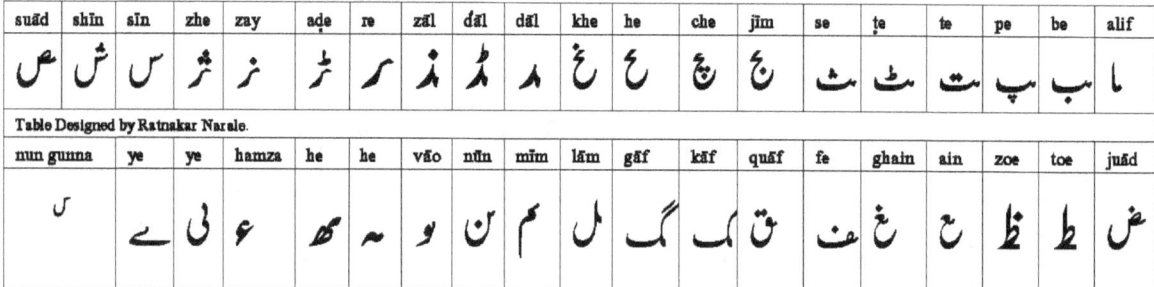

THE URDU LETTERS

(Based on Character Shapes)

GROUP 1

LESSON 3.1

The 1st letter of the Urdū Alphabet : *alif* अलिफ़ (English a Hindi अ)

ا	ـا	ـا	ا
Stand Alone	**End Position**	**Middle Position**	**Starting Positoin**

TIP 7 : (i) **No letter is connected on the LEFT SIDE of the Letter अलिफ़ *alif* (अ *a*).**

(ii) *alif* can be connected to the letter on its right side only. Therefore, in the Middle position and in End position, the shape of *alif* remains same.

Examples : Urdū name : *alif* الف (Hindi अ English *a*)

(for the letters *be* and *pe*, please see Lessons 3.2 and 3.3 or the Back Cover of the book)

(i) Letter *alif* in Stand-alone position (ا)

(ii) Letter *alif* in Starting position (ا) : **अब *ab* (now) = Right to Left ← ब b + अ a**

= ب + ا = اب (as Initial letter, *alif* अलिफ़ ا must be written in Stand-alone

shape; therefore, *be* बे ب also becomes a Stand-alone letter).

(iii) Letter *alif* in Middle position (ـا) : **बाप *bāp* (father) = Right to Left ← प *p* + a अ +**

ब b = پ + ا + ب = پ + ا + ب = باپ (*be* is written in Starting shape, *alif* in Middle position is attached to *be*, but it is detached from *pe*. Letter *pe* is written detached from *alif*, in its Stand-alone shape). See TIP 5

(iv) Letter *alif* in End position (ـا) : अब्बा *abbā* = Right to Left ← a अ ا + ब b ب + ब b ب + a अ ا = a अ ا + ब b + ब b ب + a अ ـا = ابا (*alif* ا) is in Starting shape; the first *be* ب is in Middle position and the second *be* ب is represented with a *tashdid* Marker (ّ) ; the second *alif* ا is written in End shape, which is same as its Middle position shape). See TIP 4

** TIP : Whe a consonant is doubled, the second consonant is represented by a *tashdid* Marker. For all Urdu Markers, please see LESSON 5. But, generally these Markers are skipped.

NOTE : When अलिफ़ *alif* (अ *a*) comes after the Urdū letters *dal* (د), *ḍal* (ڈ), *zal* (ذ), *re* (ر), *ade* (ڑ), *ze* (ز) and *zhe* (ژ), the *alif* is written as a Stand-alone letter. eg。 دا

ڈا ذا را ڑا زا ژا

NOTE : PLEASE DO NOT GO TO NEXT LESSONS , WITHOUT UNDERSTANDING CURRENT LESSON PROPERLY.

LESSON 3.2

The 2nd letter of the Urdū Alphabet : *be* बे ب (English b हिंदी ब)

بـ	ـبـ	ـب	ب
Starting Positoin	Middle Position	End Position	Stand Alone

REMEMBER : बे *be* (ب), पे *pe* (پ), ते *te* (ت), टे *ṭe* (ٹ) and से *se* (ث) are first group of the five letters that can easily be identified by looking at their dots (*nuqte*).

Examples : Letter *be* (ب) Urdū name : *be* بے (Hindi ब English *b*)

(for letters 's' and 'q' please see Lessons 3.18 and 3.27 or see the back cover of the book)

(i) Letter *'be'* in Stand-alone position (ب)

(ii) Letter *'be'* in Starting position (بـ) : e.g. बस *bas* (Enough!) = Right to Left ← स *s* + ब *b* = ب + س = ـس + بـ = بس (*be* ب is in Starting position and *sīn* س is in End-position)

(iii) Letter *'be'* in Middle position (ـبـ) : e.g. सबक़ *sabaq* (Lesson) = Right to Left ←क़ *q* + ब *b* + स *s* =

ق + ب + س = ـق + ـبـ + سـ = سبق (*sīn* س is written in Starting shape, *be* ب is written in 'Middle shape' and *qāf* ق is written in End shape).

(iv) Letter *'be'* in End position (ـب) : e.g. सब *sab* (All) Right to Left ← *b* ब + *s* स =

ب + س = ـب + سـ = سب (*sīn* س is in Starting shape and *be* ب is written in End shape).

EXERCISE *mashq* (مشق मश्क) 3 :

1. Read the following Urdū words and write them several times :

اب   سبق   سب   بس

2. Write the following words in Urdū :

अब *ab* (Now), सबक़ *sabaq* (Lesson), सब *sab*, (All), बस *bas* (Enough!)

LESSON 3.3

The 3rd letter of the Urdū Alphabet : *pe* पे پ (English p हिंदी प)

پ	ـپ	ـپـ	پـ
Stand Alone	End Position	Middle Position	Starting Positoin

Examples : Letter *pe* (پ) Urdū name *pe* پے) (Hindi प English *p*)

NOTE : for the additional letters *re* ڑ and *che* چ please see Lessons 3.14 and 3.3, or please see the back cover of the book

(i) Letter *'pe'* in Stand-alone position (پ)

(ii) Letter *'pe'* in Starting position (پ) : e.g. पर *par* (Wing) Right to Left ← र *r* + प *p*

= ر ب += ر + پ = پر (*pe* پ is in Starting position and letter *re* ر is in End-position)

(iii) Letter *'pe'* in Middle position (پ) : e.g. चपत *chapat* (a slap) Right to Left ← t त + p प + ch च = چ + پ + ت = ت + پ + چ = چپت (*che* چ is written in Starting shape, *pe* پ is written in 'Middle shape' and *te* ت is written in End shape.

(iv) Letter *'pe'* in End position (پ) : e.g. तप *tap* (Feaver, Heat) Right to Left ← प *p* + त *t* = ت + پ = پ + ت = تپ (*te* ت is written in Starting shape, and *pe* پ is written in End shape.

EXERCISE *mashq* (مشق मश्क) 4 :

1. Read the following Urdū words and write them several times :

ر بابا بابا پ باپ

2. Write the following words in Urdū :

बाबा (*bābā*, Grand-father), पापा (*pāpā*, Father), सबक़ (*sabaq*, Lesson).

LESSON 3.4

The 4th letter of the Urdū Alphabet : *te* ते ت (English t हिंदी त)

Nastā'leeq style :

ت ـت ـتـ تـ

Stand Alone End Position Middle Position Starting Positoin

NOTE : This the first त *'t'* sound

(see टे *ṭe* ٹ in Lesson 3.5, तोए *toe* ط in Lesson 3.22)

Examples : Letter *te* (ت) Urdū name *te* تے (Hindi त English *t*)

(i) Letter *'te'* in Stand-alone position (ت)

(ii) Letter *'te'* in Starting position (تـ) : e.g. तप *tap* (Feaver, Heat) Right to Left ← प *p* + त *t* =

ت + پ = ـپ + تـ = تپ (*te* ب is written in Starting shape, and *pe* پ is written in End shape.

(iii) Letter *'te'* in Middle position (ـتـ) : e.g. क़त्ल *qtla* (Slaughter) Right to Left ← *l* ल + t त् + q क़ = ل + ت + ق = ـل + ـتـ + قـ = قتل (*qāf* ق is written in Starting shape, *te* ت is written in 'Middle shape' and *lām* ل is written in End shape).

NOTE : Please see letter लाम *lām* ل in Lesson 3.30

(iv) Letter *'te'* in End position (ـت): e.g.

(1) बत *bat* (Bird) Right to Left ← *t* त + *b* ब = ب + ت = ـت + بـ =

بت (*be* بـ is written in Starting shape, and *te* ـت is in End shape).

Similarly,

(2) बात *bāt* (thing, story) Right to Left ← t त + bā बा = با + ت = بات (*bā*

बा با is written in Starting shape as said in Lesson 3.1 and *te* ـت is written in End

shape).

EXERCISE *mashq* (مشق मश्क) 5 :

1. Read the following Urdū words and write them several times :

اب بب بات تب

2. Write the following words in Urdū :

अब *ab* (Now), बात *bāt* (Abstract thing, matter), तब *tab* (Then).

LESSON 3.5

The 5th letter of the Urdū Alphabet : *ṭe* टे ٹ (English *ṭ* हिंदी ट)

ٹ ـٹ ـٹـ ٹـ

Stand Alone **End Position** **Middle Position** **Starting Positoin**

NOTE : This the second Urdu त (ट) *'t'* sound

(see ते *te* ت Lesson 3.4 and तोए *toe* ط Lesson 3.22)

Examples : Letter ***ṭe*** (ٹ) Urdu namē *ṭe* ٹے **(Hindi ट English phonetic *ṭ*)**

(for letters '*kāf*' and '*lām*' please see Lessons 3.28 and 3.30, or see the back cover of the book)

(i) Letter *'ṭe'* in Stand-alone position (ٹ)

(ii) Letter *'ṭe'* in Starting position : **e.g. टप *ṭap* (Tap! sound) Right to Left ← प *p* + ट**

ṭ = پ + ٹ = ـپ + ٹـ = ٹپ (*ṭe* is in Starting position and *pe* is in End-position).

(iii) Letter *'ṭe'* in Middle position : **e.g. पटक् *paṭak* (to Drop) Right to Left ← k क + ṭ**

ट+ p प = ک + ٹ + پ = ـک + ـٹـ + پـ = پٹک (*pe* is written in Starting shape, *ṭe* is written in 'Middle shape' and *kāf* is written in End shape).

(iv) Letter *'ṭe'* in End position : **e.g. पलट *palaṭ* (To turn. return) Right to Left ← ṭ ट**

+ +1ल + pप = ٹ + ل + پ = ـٹ + ـلـ + پـ = پلٹ

(*pe* is written in Starting shape, *lām* is in 'Middle Shape' and *ṭe* is written in End shape).

EXERCISE *mashq* (مشق मश्क) 6 :

1. Read the following Urdū words and write them several times :

لپٹ   بلا   لٹک   سب

2. Write the following words in Urdū :

सब ***sab*** **(All), बला** ***balā*** **(Super), लटक** ***laṭak*** **(Hang), लपट** ***lapat*** **(Flame)**

LESSON 3.6

The 6th letter of the Urdū Alphabet : *se* से ث (English S हिंदी स)

ث	ـث	ـثـ	ثـ
Stand Alone	**End Position**	**Middle Position**	**Starting Positoin**

NOTE 1 : This the first स '*s*' sound (see सीन *sīn* 3.18, शीन *shīn* 3.19 and सुआद *suād* 3.20)

NOTE 2 : **This से *se* (ث) is the LEAST USED 's' type of sound in Urdū language**

Examples : Letter *se* (ث) Urdū name *se* ثے (Hindi स English *s*)

(for letters *mīm* and *re* please see Lessons 31 and 14, or see the back cover of the book)

(i) Letter *'se'* in Stand-alone position (ث)

(ii) Letter *'se'* in Starting position : e.g. समर *samar* (Fruit) Right to Left ← र *r* + *m* म

+ स *s* = ر + م + ث = ر + مـ + ثـ = ثمر (*se* ث is in Starting

position, *mīm* م is in Middle position and letter *re* ر is in End-position).

(iii) Letter *'se'* in Middle position : e.g. असर *asar* (Effect) Right to Left ← र r + स *s*

+ अ *a* = ر + ث + ا = ر + ثـ + ا = اثر (*alif* ا is written in

Starting shape, *se* ث is written in 'Middle shape' and *re* ر is written in End shape).

(iv) Letter *'se'* in End position : e.g. सालस, सालिस *sālis* (Mediator) Right to Left ← स

s + + ल *l* + सा *sā* = ث + ل + ا = ث + ل + ا + ثـ = ثالث

(*se* ث is written in Starting shape, *alif* ا and *lām* ل are in 'Middle Shape' and the second *se* is written in End shape).

EXERCISE *mashq* (مشق मश्क) 7 :

1. Read the following Urdū words and write them several times :

باب اب عرب ترب

2. Write the following words in Urdū : अब *ab* (Now), तरब *tarab* (Joy)

URDU LETTERS GROUP 2 (based on Character Shapes)

LESSON 3.7

The 7th letter of the Urdū Alphabet : ***jīm*** जीम ج (***English*** **j** **हिंदी ज**)

ج	ـج	ـجـ	جـ
Stand Alone	**End Position**	**Middle Position**	**Starting Positoin**

NOTE : This is the first ज *'j'* sound

(see : ज़ाल *jāl* ذ in Lesson 3.13, झे ژ *je* in Lesson 3.16, ज़े *ze* ز in Lesson 3.17,

ज़ुआद *juād* ض in Lesson 3.21 and ज़ोए ظ *joe* in Lesson 3.23)

REMEMBER : **जीम *jīm* (ج), चे *che* (چ), हे *he* (ح) and खे *khe* (خ) is second group of letters which can be identified simply by looking at the dots (*nuqte*).**

Examples : जीम *jīm* (ج) Urdū name *jīm* جیم (Hindi ज English *j*)

(i) Letter *'jīm'* in Stand-alone position (ج)

(ii) Letter *'jīm'* in Starting position (جـ) : **e.g. जब *jab* (When) Right to Left ← ब *b* +**

जज *j* = ب + ج = بـ + جـ = جب (*jīm* ج is in Starting position and *be* ب is in End-position).

(iii) Letter *'jīm'* in Middle position (ـجـ) : e.g. बजा *bajā* (Proper, right) Right to Left ←

अ *a* + ज *j* + ब *b* = ا + ج + ب = ـا + ـجـ + بـ = بجا (*be* ب is written in Starting shape, *jīm* ج is written in 'Middle shape' and *alif* ا is written in End shape).

(iv) Letter *'jīm'* in End position (ـج) : e.g. हज *haj* (A pilgrimage) Right to Left ← ज *j* + ह *h* =

ج + ح = ـج + حـ = حج (*he* ح is written in Starting shape and *jīm* ج is in End shape).

EXERCISE *mashq* (مشق मश्क) 8 :

1. Read the following Urdū words and write them several times :

حب بجا سجا رجا ٓاا ٓاب

2. Write the following words in Urdū :

जब *jab* (When), सज़ा *sajā* (Punishment), रज़ा *rajā* (Expectation), रजा *rajā (Hope)*.

LESSON 3.8

The 8th letter of the Urdū Alphabet : *che* चे چ (English ch हिंदी च)

چ	ـچ	ـچـ	چـ
Stand Alone	**End Position**	**Middle Position**	**Starting Positoin**

Examples : चे *che* (چ) : Urdū name *che* چے (हिंदी च English *ch*)

(i) Letter *'che'* in Stand-alone position (چ)

(ii) Letter *'che'* in Starting position (چـ) : e.g. चचा *chachā* (Uncle) Right to Left ←

अ *a* + च *ch* + च *ch* = ا + چ + چ = ـا + ـچـ + چـ = چچا (**first**

che **چ is in Starting position, another *che* is in Middle shape and *alif* is in End-position).**

(iii) Letter *'che'* in Middle position (ـچـ) : **See the example given above, चचा *chachā* (Uncle).**

Notice the difference between Starting (چـ) and Middle (ـچـ) shapes of *che* چ in this example.

(iv) Letter *'che'* in End position (ـچ) : e.g. सच ***sach*** (True) Right to Left ← च ***ch*** + स ***s*** =

چ + س = ـچ + سـ = سچ (***sīn*** س **is written in Starting shape, and *che*** چ

is in End shape).

EXERCISE *mashq* (مشق मश्क) 9 :

1. Read the following Urdū words and write them several times :

سچ حا بچ حل

2. Write the following words in Urdū :

सच *sach* (True), चल *chal* (Walk), बच *bach* (Remain, to get saved).

LESSON 3.9

The 9th letter of the Urdū Alphabet : ***he*** हे ح (English h हिंदी ह)

ح	ـح	ـحـ	حـ
Stand Alone	End Position	Middle Position	Starting Positoin

NOTE : This is the first ह *'h'* sound (see : छोटी हे *chhoṭī he* Lesson 3.34 and दो चश्मी हे *do chashmī he* ھ is in Lesson 3.5

Examples : हे *he* (ح) : Urdū name *he* حے (हिंदी ह English *h*)

(i) Letter *'he'* in Stand-alone position (ح)

(ii) Letter *'he'* in Starting position (حـ) : e.g. हल *hal* (Plough) Right to Left ← ल *l* +

ह *h* = ل + ح = ل + حـ = حل (*he* ح is in Starting and *lām* ل is in End-shape).

(iii) Letter *'he'* in Middle position (ـحـ) : e.g. बहाल *bahāl* (Reinstate) Right to Left ←

ल *l*+ अ *a*+ ह h + ब *b* = ل + ا + ح + ب = ل + ـا + ـحـ + بـ = بحال

(*be* ب is in Starting position, *badi he* ح is in Middle shape, *alif* is in Middle position and *jām* ل is in End-shape).

(iv) Letter *'he'* in End position (ـح) : e.g. सुबह, सबह *subah* (Morning) Right to Left

← ह *h* + ब *b* + उ *u*+ स *s* (सु *su*) = ہ + ب + و + ص = ـہ + ـبـ + ـو

+ صـ = صوبہ (*suād* ص is written in Starting shape, *vāo* و is written in Middle shape, *be* ب is also in Middle shape and *choti he* ہ is written in End shape).

EXERCISE *mashq* (مشق मश्क) 10 :

1. Read the following Urdū words and write them several times :

مہک صبح محل سچ

2. Write the following words in Urdū - :

महल *mahal* (Palace), महक *mahak, mehek* (Fragrance), सच *sach* (True), सुबह *subah* (Morning)

LESSON 3.10

The 10th letter of the Urdū Alphabet : *khe* खे خ (English kh हिंदी ख़)

خ	ـخ	ـخـ	خـ
Stand Alone	**End Position**	**Middle Position**	**Starting Positoin**

Examples : ख़े ***khe*** (خ) : Urdū name ***khe*** خے (Hindi ख़ English *kh*)

(i) Letter *'khe'* in Stand-alone position (خ) :

(ii) Letter *'khe'* in Starting position (خـ) : e.g. ख़ता ***khatā*** (Fault) Right to Left ← अ ***a***

+ त *t* + ख़ *kh* = ا + ط + خ = ـا + ـطـ + خـ = خطا (***khe*** خ is in

Starting position, *toe* ط is in Middle shape and *alif* is in End-shape).

(iii) Letter *'khe'* in Middle position (ـخـ) : e.g. तख़्त ***takhta*** (Throne) Right to Left ←

त *t*+ ख़् *kh* + त *t* = ت + خ + ت = ـت + ـخـ + تـ = تخت

(***te*** **is in Starting position, *khe* is in Middle shape and second *te* is in End-shape).**

(iv) Letter *'khe'* in End position (ـخ) : e.g. तलख़ ***talkh*** (Bitter) Right to Left ← ख़ ***ka***

+ ल *l* + त *t* = خ + ل + ت = خ + لـ + تـ = تلخ (*te* is written in Starting shape, *lām* is in Middle shape and *khe* is written in End shape).

EXERCISE *mashq* (مشق मश्क) **11 :**

1. Read the following Urdū words and write them several times :

ختم خطا سب ب ب خبر

2. Write the following words in Urdū :

खता *Khatā* (Fault), **ख़बर** *khabar* (News), **सब** *sab* (All), **तब** *tab* (Then)

URDU LETTERS GROUP 3 (based on Character Shapes)

LESSON 3.11

The 11th letter of the Urdū Alphabet : *dāl* दाल د (English d हिंदी द)

د	ـد	ـد	د
Stand Alone	**End Position**	**Middle Position**	**Starting Positoin**

NOTE : This is the first द *'d'* type of sound

(see : डाल *ḍāl* Lesson 3.12 and अड़े *aḍe* Lesson 3.15)

REMEMBER :

(1) **Letters दाल *dāl* (د), डाल *ḍāl* (ڈ), ज़ाल *jāl* (ذ); रे *re* (ر), अड़े *aḍe* (ڑ), ज़े *zay* (ز)**

and ज्ये *zhe* (ژ) is the third group of letters which can be identified simply by looking at the dots (*nuqte*).

<u>Examples</u> : दाल *dāl* (د) : Urdū name *dāl* دال (हिंदी द English *d*)

(i) <u>Letter *'dāl'* in Stand-alone position</u> (د)

(ii) <u>Letter *dāl* in Starting position</u> (د) **: e.g. दर्द *dard* (Pain) Right to Left ← द *d* + र *r* + द *d* =**

د + ر + د = د + ر + د = درد **(*dāl* د is in Starting and End positions and *re* ر is in Middle) See TIP 3**

(iii) <u>Letter *'dāl'* in Middle position</u> (ـد) **: e.g. बदल *badal* (Change) Right to Left ←**

ल *l* + द *d* + ब *b* = ل + د + ب = ل + ـد + بـ = بدل **(*be***

ب **is in Starting position, *dāl* د is in Middle shape and *lām* ل is in End-shape).**

(iv) <u>Letter *'dāl'* in End position</u> (ـد) **: e.g. बद *bad* (Bad) Right to Left ← द *d* + ब *b* =**

د + ب = د + بـ = بد (*be* ب is written as in Starting shape, *dāl* د is in End shape). See TIP 4

EXERCISE *mashq* (مشق मश्क) **12 :**

1. Read the following Urdū words and write them several times :

درد بد دس بدل ادا ادب

2. Write the following words in Urdū :

अदा *adā* (To present), **खबर** *khabar* (News), **बदल** *badal* (To change), **बात** *bāt* (thing, matter)

LESSON 3.12

The 12th letter of the Urdū Alphabet : *ḍāl* डाल ڈ (English ḍ हिंदी ड)

ڈ	ـڈ	ـڈ	ڈ
Stand Alone	**End Position**	**Middle Position**	**Starting Positoin**

NOTE : This is the second द *'d'* type of sound (see : दाल *dāl* lesson 3.11 and अड़े *aḍe* lesson 3.15)

Examples : डाल *ḍāl* (ڈ) : Urdū name *ḍāl* ڈال (हिंदी ड English *ḍ* Phonetic)

(i) Letter *'ḍāl'* in Stand-alone position (ڈ)

(ii) Letter *'ḍāl'* in Starting position (ڈ) : e.g. **डर** *ḍar* (Fear) Right to Left ← र *r* + ड

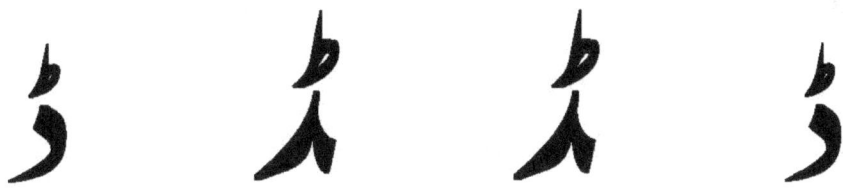

ḍ = ر + ڈ = ر + ڈ = ڈر (*ḍāl* is in Starting letter and *re* is End-letter, but in Stand-alone shape). See TIP 2

(iii) Letter *'ḍāl'* in Middle position (ڈ) : e.g. अंडा *anḍā* (Egg) Right to Left ← अ *a* + ड *ḍ* + न *n* + अ *a* = ا + ڈ + ن + ا = ا + ڈ + ن + ا =

انڈا (first *alif* is in Starting position, *nūn* is in Middle, *ḍāl* is also in Middle shape and another *alif* is in End-shape).

(iv) Letter *'ḍāl'* in End position (ڈ) : e.g. साँड *sānḍ* (Bull) Right to Left ← ड *ḍ* + न *n* + अ *a* + स *s* = ڈ + ن + ا + س = ڈ + ن + ا + س =

سانڈ (*sīn* is in Starting shape, *alif* is in Middle shape, *nūn* is in Middle shape and *ḍāl* is in End shape).

EXERCISE *mashq* (مشق मश्क) 13 :

1. Read the following Urdū words and write them several times :

انڈا ڈر ڈاکٹر ڈب

2. Write the following words in Urdū :

डर *ḍar* (Fear), डट *ḍat* (Be steady), अंडा *anḍā* (Egg), बात *bāt* (Thing)

LESSON 3.13

The 13th letter of the Urdū Alphabet : *zāl* ज़ाल ذ (English Z हिंदी ज़)

ذ ـذ ـذ ذ

Stand Alone **End Position** **Middle Position** **Starting Positoin**

NOTE : This is the second ज *'j'* sound (see : जीम *jīm* in Lesson 3.7, ज़े *je* in Lesson 3.16, ज़े *je* in Lesson 3.17, ज़ुआद *juād* in Lesson 3.21 and ज़ोए *joe* in Lesson 3.23)

Examples : ज़ाल *zāl* (ذ) : Urdū name *jāl* ذال (हिंदी ज़ English *j*)

(i) Letter *'zāl'* in Stand-alone position (ذ)

(ii) Letter *'zāl'* in Starting position (ذ) : **e.g. ज़रा *jarā* (a bit) Right to Left ← अ *m* + र *d* + ज़ *z* =**

ا + ر + ذ = ا + ر + ذ = ذرا **(*zāl* ذ is in Starting position, *re* ر is in Middle position but Stand alone and *alif* is in End-shape but Stand alone position) See TIP 4.**

(iii) Letter *'jāl'* in Middle position (ـذ) : **e.g. जज़र *jajar* (Slope, lessening) Right to Left ← र *r* + ज़ *j* + ज *j* = ر + ذ + ج = ـر + ـذ + جـ = جذر (*jīm* ج is in Starting position, *zāl* ذ is in Middle shape and *re* ر is in End-shape as if** detached),

(iv) Letter *'jāl'* in End position (ز) : e.g. मग्ज़ *magz* (Brain) Right to Left ← ज़ *z* + ग् *g* + म *m* =

ز + غ + م = ز + غ + م = مغز (*mīm* م is in Starting shape, *gain* غ is in Middle shape and *zāl* ز is in End shape).

EXERCISE *mashq* (مشق मश्क) 14 :

1. Read the following Urdū words and write them several times :

مغز   جزر   س   س   رر

2. Write the following words in Urdū :

तब *tab* (Then), डर *ḍar* (Fear), अंडा *anḍā* (Egg)

LESSON 3.14

The 14th letter of the Urdū Alphabet : *re* रे ر (English r हिंदी र)

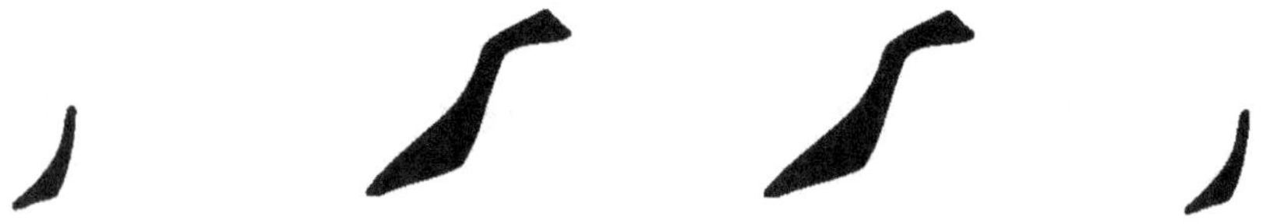

Stand Alone | End Position | Middle Position | Starting Positoin

Examples : रे *re* (ر) : Urdū name *re* رے (Hindi र English *r*)

(i) Letter *'re'* in Stand-alone position (ر)

(ii) Letter *'re'* in Starting position (ر) : e.g. रब *rab* (God) Right to Left ← ब *b* + र *r*

= ب + ر = ب + ر = رب (*re* is in Starting shape, *be* is in End-shape). See TIP 2

(iii) Letter *'re'* in Middle position (ر) : e.g. चरम *charam* (Skin) Right to Left ← म *m* + र *r* + च *ch* = م + ر + ح = م + ر + چ = چرم (*jīm* ح is in Starting position, *re* ر is in Middle shape and *mīm* م is in End-shape). See TIP 3

(iv) Letter *'re'* in End position (ر) : e.g. पर *par* (Wing) Right to Left ← र *r* + प *p* = ر + پ = پ + ر = پر (*pe* is in Starting shape, nd *re* is in End shape).

EXERCISE *mashq* (مشق मश्क) 15 :

1. Read the following Urdū words and write them several times :

سر ڈر رب چرم

2. Write the following words in Urdū :

डर *ḍar* (Fear), सब *sab* (All), पर *par* (Wing), तब *tab* (Then)

LESSON 3.15

The 15th letter of the Urdū Alphabet : *aḍe* अड़े ڑ (English ḍ हिंदी ड़)

ڑ	ڑ	ڑ	(Does not apply)
Stand Alone	**End Position**	**Middle Position**	**Starting Positoin**

NOTE : This is the third द *'d'* type of sound (see : दाल *dāl* 3.11 and डाल *ḍāl* 3.12)

Examples : अड़े *aḍe* (ڑ) : Urdū name *aḍe* اڑے (हिंदी ड़ English *ḍ*)

(i) Letter *'aḍe'* in Stand-alone position (ڑ)

(ii) Letter *'aḍe'* in Starting position (ڑ) : **Urdū and Hindi words do not start with letter *aḍe* ڑ.**

(iii) Letter *'aḍe'* in Middle position (ڑ) : **e.g. बड़ा *baḍā* (Big) Right to Left ← अ *a* + ड़ *ḍ* + ब *b*** = ا + ڑ + ب = ا + ڑ + ب = بڑا **(*be* ب is in Starting position, *aḍe* ڑ is in Middle shape and *alif* is in End-shape).**

(iv) Letter *'aḍe'* in End position (ڑ) : **e.g. जड़ *jaḍ* (Root) Right to Left ← ड़ *ḍ* + ज *j*** = ڑ + ج = ڑ + ج = جڑ **(*jīm* ج is in Starting shape, *aḍe* ڑ is in End shape)**

EXERCISE *mashq* (مشق मश्क) **16 :**

1. Read the following Urdū words and write them several times :

ج ح ب بڑا اب

2. Write the following words in Urdū :

अब *ab* (Now), **बड़ा** (*baḍā* (Big)

LESSON 3.16

The 16th letter of the Urdū Alphabet : *zay* ज़े ز (English jh हिंदी झ, ज़)

ز ز ز ز

Stand Alone **End Position** **Middle Position** **Starting Positoin**

NOTE : This is the second ज *'j'* sound (see : जीम *jīm* in Lesson 3.7, ज़े *je* in Lesson 3.16, ज़े *je* in Lesson 3.17, ज़ुआद *juād* in Lesson 3.21 and ज़ोए *joe* in Lesson 3.23)

NOTE 2 : **This ज़े, झे *zay, ze* (ز) is**

the MOST USED 'j' type of sound in Urdū language

Examples : ज़े *zay* (ز) : Urdū name *zay* زے (Hindi झ, ज़ English *z*)

(for letter nūn (न *na*) see lesson 3.32 and for letter qāf (क़ q) see lesson 3.27)

(i) Letter *'zay'* in Stand-alone position (ز)

(ii) Letter *'zay'* in Starting position (ز) : e.g. ज़बर *zabar* (Superior, larger) Right to Left ← र *r* + ब *b* + ज़ *z* = ر + ب + ز = ر + ب + ز = زبر (*zay* is in Starting shape, *be* is in Middle shape and letter *re* is in End-shape).

(iii) Letter *'zay'* in Middle position (ز) : e.g. बाज़ार *bāzār* (Market) Right to Left ← बा *bā* + ज़ा *zā* + र *r* = ر + زا + با = بازار (*be* is in Starting position with *alif*. *zay* is in starting position with alif and *re* is in End-shape).

(iv) Letter *'zay'* in End position (ز) : e.g. जहाज़ *jahāz* (Constipation) Right to Left ← ज़ *z* + अ *a* + ह *h* + ज *j* = ز + ا + ہ + ج = ز + ا + ہ + ج = جہاز (*jīm* ج is in Starting shape, *choti he* ہ is in Middle shape, *alif* is in Middle position and *zay* ز is in End shape).

EXERCISE *mashq* (مشق मश्क) 17 :

1. Read the following Urdū words and write them several times :

جہاز زر راز ساز جہاز

2. Write the following words in Urdū :

क़ब्ज़ *qbz* (Constipation), साज़ *sāz* (Music), ज़रब *zarab* (Stroke)

LESSON 3.17

The 17th letter of the Urdū Alphabet : *zhe* ज़े ژ (English zh हिंदी ज़्य)

ژ	ـژ	ـژ	ژ
Stand Alone	**End Position**	**Middle Position**	**Starting Positoin**

NOTE : This is the second ज *'j'* sound (see : जीम *jīm* in Lesson 3.7, ज़े *je* in Lesson 3.16, ज़े *je* in Lesson 3.17, ज़ुआद *juād* in Lesson 3.21 and ज़ोए *joe* in Lesson 3.23)

NOTE 2 : **This ज़्ये *zhe* (ژ) is the least used 'j' type of sound in Urdū language**

Examples : झ्ये *zhe* (ژ) : Urdū name *zhe* ژے (Hindi ज़्य Eng. *zh*)

(i) Letter *'zhe'* in Stand-alone position (ژ)

(ii) Letter *'zhe'* in Starting position (ژ) : **e.g. ज़्याल (ज़्याल:) *zhal* (Hail) Right to**

Left ← ल *l* + अ *a* + ज़्य *zh* = ل + ا + ژ = ل + ـا + ژ = ژال

(*zhe* ژ is in Starting shape, *alif* is in Middle shape and letter *lām* ل is in End-shape, as if Stand alone) see TIP 4.

(iii) Letter *'zhe'* in Middle position (ژ) : e.g. मज़्यब (मुज़िब) *muzhib* (Melting)

Right to Left ← ब *b* + ज़ *zh* + म *m* = ب + ژ + م = ب + ژ + م = مژب (*mīm* م is in Starting position, *zhe* ژ is in Middle shape and *be* ب is in End-shape).

(iv) Letter *'zhe'* in End position (ژ) : e.g. कज़ *kazh* (Bent, crooked; silk) Right to Left ← ज़ *zh* + क *k* = ژ + ک = ژ + ک = کژ (*kāf* ک is in Starting shape, and *zhe* ژ is in End shape).

EXERCISE *mashq* (مشق मश्क) 18 :

1. Read the following Urdū words and write them several times :

بس   حب   بجا   سجا

2. Write the following words in Urdū :

कब्ज़ *qbz* (Constipation), साज़ *sāz* (Music), जब *jab* (When), कब *kab* (When?)

URDU LETTERS GROUP 4 (based on Character Shapes)

LESSON 3.18

The 18th letter of the Urdū Alphabet : *sīn* सीन س (English S हिंदी स)

س	س	ـسـ	سـ
Stand Alone	**End Position**	**Middle Position**	**Starting Positoin**

NOTE : This is the second स *'s'* sound (look : से *se* in Lesson 3.16, शीन *shīn* Lesson 3.19 and सुआद *suād* Lesson 3.20)

REMEMBER : **Letters सीन *sīn* (س) and शीन *shīn* (ش), सुआद *suād* (ص) and जुआद *juād* (ض) is the fourth group of letters which can be identified simply by looking at the dots (*nuqte*).**

Examples : सीन *sīn* (س) : Urdū name *sīn* سین (हिंदी स English *s*)

(i) Letter *'sīn'* in Stand-alone position (س)

(ii) Letter *'sīn'* in Starting position (سـ) : **e.g. सब *sab* (All) Right to Left ← ब *b* +**

स *s* = ب + س = ب + سـ = سب (***sīn* is in Starting shape,**

and *be* is in the End-shape).

(iii) Letter *'sīn'* in Middle position (ـسـ) : **e.g. बसर *basar* (Maintenance) Right to Left**

←र *r* + स् *s* + ब *b* = ر + س + ب = ـر + ـسـ + بـ = بسر (*be*

ب is in Starting position, *sīn* س is in Middle shape. *re* ر is in End-shape).

(iv) Letter *'sīn'* in End position (ـس) : **e.g. बस *bas* (Enough!) Right to Left ← स *s* +**

ब *b* = س + ب = ـس + بـ = بس (*be* **is in Starting shape, and *sīn* is in**

End shape).

EXERCISE *mashq* (مشق मश्क) 19 :

1. Read the following Urdū words and write them several times :

بس سب بسر

2. Write the following words in Urdū :

सस्ता *sastā* (Cheap), बस्ता *bastā* (Bag), सब *sab* (All), बस *bas* (Enough!)

LESSON 3.19

The 19th letter of the Urdū Alphabet : *shīn* शीन ش (English sh हिंदी श)

ش	ـش	ـشـ	شـ
Stand Alone	**End Position**	**Middle Position**	**Starting Positoin**

NOTE : This is the third स 's' sound (look : से *se* 3.8, सीन *sīn* Lesson 3.18 and सुआद *suād* Lesson 3.20)

Examples : शीन *shīn* (ش) : Urdū name *shīn* شین (हिंदी श Eng. *sh*)

(i) Letter *'shīn'* in Stand-alone position (ش)

(ii) Letter *'shīn'* in Starting position (شـ) : e.g. **शब** ***shab*** **(Night) Right to Left ← ब** ***b***

+ श ***sh*** = ب + ش = ب + شـ = شب **(*shīn* ش is in Starting shape, and *be* ب is in the End-shape).**

(iii) Letter *'shīn'* in Middle position (ـشـ) **: e.g. तश्त** ***tashta*** **(a Shallow pan) Right to**

Left ← त ***t*** **+ श्** ***sh*** **+ त** ***t*** = ت + ش + ت = ـت + ـشـ + تـ

= تشت **(first *te* ت is in Starting position, *shīn* ش is in Middle shape, and the last *te* ت is in End-shape).**

(iv) Letter *'shīn'* in End position (ـش) **: e.g. कश** ***kash*** **(Puff) Right to Left ← श** ***sh*** **+**

क ***k*** = ش + ک = ـش + کـ = کش **(*kāf* ک is in Starting shape, and *shīn* ش is in End shape).**

EXERCISE *mashq* (مشق मश्क) 20 :

1. Read the following Urdū words and write them several times :

مالش سس سس پلٹ

2. Write the following words in Urdū :

मालश, मालश *mālish* (Massage), बस्ता *bastā* (Bag), पलट *palat* (To turn), अंडा *anḍā* (Egg)

LESSON 3.20

The 20th letter of the Urdū Alphabet : *suād* सुआद ص (English S हिंदी स)

ص	ـص	ـصـ	صـ
Stand Alone	**End Position**	**Middle Position**	**Starting Positoin**

NOTE : This is the fourth स *'s'* sound (See : से *se* Lesson 3.8, सीन *sīn* Lesson 3.18 and शीन *shīn* Lesson 3.19)

Examples : सुआद *suād* (ص) : Urdū name *suād* صاد (हिंदी स Eng. *s*)

(i) Letter *'suād'* in Stand-alone position (ص)

(ii) Letter *'suād'* in Starting position (صـ) : e.g. **सद *sad* (One Hundred) Right to Left**

← द *d* + स *s* = د + ص = ـد + صـ = صد (*suād* ص **is in Starting shape and *dāl* د is in the End-shape).**

(iii) Letter *'suād'* in Middle position (ـصـ) : e.g. **बसर *basar* (Vision, sight) Right to**

Left ← र *r* + स *s* + ब *b* = ر + ص + ب = ـر + ـصـ + بـ =

بصر (*be* ب in Starting position, *suād* ص in Middle shape and *re* ر in End-shape).

(iv) Letter *'suād'* in End position (ص) : e.g. मख़्लस (मुख़लिस) ***makhlas (mukhlis)***

(Honest, natural, truthful) Right to Left ← स *s* + ल *l* + ख *kh* + म *m* = ص +

ل + م + خ = ص + ـلـ + ـخـ + مـ = مخلص (*mīm* م is in

Starting shape, ***khe*** خ is in Middle position, ***lām*** ل is in Middle position and ***suād***

ص is in End shape).

EXERCISE *mashq* (مشق मश्क) 21 :

1. Read the following Urdū words and write them several times :

بس سب صد مخلص

2. Write the following words in Urdū :

बसर *basar* (Livelyhood), मुख़लिस, मख़्लिस *makhlas* (Honest), बस *bas* (Enough!), सच *sach* (Truth)

LESSON 3.21

The 21st letter of the Urdū Alphabet : *juād* जुआद ض (English j हिंदी ज)

ض ـض ـضـ ضـ

Stand Alone **End Position** **Middle Position** **Starting Positoin**

NOTE : This is the second ज *'j'* sound (see : जीम *jīm* in Lesson 3.7, ज़े *je* in Lesson 3.16, ज़े *je* in Lesson 3.17, जुआद *juād* in Lesson 3.21 and ज़ोए *joe* in Lesson 3.23)

Examples : **जुआद** ***juād*** (ض) : Urdū name ***juad*** **صاد** **(हिंदी ज Eng. *j*)**

(i) Letter *'juād'* in Stand-alone position (ض)

(ii) Letter *'juād'* in Starting position (ضـ) : **e.g. ज़मानत *zamānat* (Surety, Bail) Right to Left ←** त *t* + न *n* + अ *a* + म *m* + ज़ *za* = ت + ن + ا + م +

ض = ـت + ـنـ + ـا + ـمـ + ضـ = ضمانت (*juād* ض **is in Starting shape, *mīm* م is in the Middle-shape, *alif* ا is in the Middle-shape, *nūn* ن is in the Middle-shape, and *te* ت is in End shape) see TIP 4.**

(iii) Letter *'juād'* in Middle position (ـضـ) : **e.g. हज़ूर *huzūr* (Sir) Right to Left ← र *r***

+ ज़ू *zu* + ह *h* = ر + و + ض + ح = ر + و + ضـ + حـ = حضور (*he* ح is in Starting position, *juād* ض and *vāO* و are in Middle shape; and *re* ر is in End-Stand-alone shape).

(iv) Letter *'juād'* in End position (ض) : e.g. क़बज *kabaj* (Stomach ache) Right to Left ← ज *xj* + ब *b* + क़ *k* = ض + ب + ق = ض + بـ + قـ = قبض (*qāf* is in Starting shape, *be* is in Middle position and *juād* is in End shape).

EXERCISE *mashq* (مشق मश्क) 22 :

1. Read the following Urdū words and write them several times :

مرض   قبض   اب ذرہ

2. Write the following words in Urdū :

ज़रा *zarā* (A bit, little), मरज़ *maraz* (Sickness), कबज़ *qabaz* (Stomach ailment), पर *par* (Wing)

URDU LETTERS GROUP 5 (based on Character Shapes)

LESSON 3.22

The 22nd letter of the Urdū Alphabet : *toe* तोए ط (English t हिंदी त)

ط	ـط	ـطـ	طـ
Stand Alone	**End Position**	**Middle Position**	**Starting Positoin**

NOTE : This is the third त *'t'* sound

(see ते *te* Lesson 3.4 and टे *ṭe* Lesson 3.25)

REMEMBER :

Letters तोए *toe* (ط), ज़ोए *zoe* (ظ); ऐन *ain* (ع), गैन *gain* (غ); and फ़े *fe* (ف), काफ़ *qāf* (ق) are the fifth group of letters which can be identified simply by looking at their dots (*nuqte*).

Examples : तोए *toe* (ط) : Urdū name *toe* طوے (हिंदी त Eng. *t*)

(i) Letter *'toe'* in Stand-alone position (ط) :

(ii) Letter *'toe'* in Starting position (طـ) : **e.g. तलब *talab* (Desire, addiction) Right** to Left ← ब *b* + ल *l* + त *t* = ب + ل + ط = ب + لـ + طـ =

طلب (*toe* ط is in Starting shape, *lām* ل is in Middle position and *be* ب is in End position).

(iii) Letter *'toe'* in Middle position (ـطـ) : e.g. बत्तख़ *battakh* (Duck) Right to Left ←

ख़ *kh* + त *t* + ब *b* = خ + ط + ب = خ + ـطـ + بـ = بطخ (*te*

ب is in Starting position, *toe* ط is in Middle shape. *khe* خ is in End-shape).

(iv) Letter *'toe'* in End position (ـط) : e.g. ख़त *khat* (Letter) Right to Left ← त *t*

+ ख़ *kh* = ط + خ = ـط + خـ = خط (*khe* خ is in Starting shape, and

toe ط is in End shape).

EXERCISE *mashq* (مشق मश्क) 23 :

1. Read the following Urdū words and write them several times :

طلب بط ب بطخ خط

2. Write the following words in Urdū :

बतख़ *batakh* (Duck), तब *tab* (Then), क़बज़ *qabaj* (Constipation), तलब *talab* (Desire)

LESSON 3.23

The 23rd letter of the Urdū Alphabet : *zoe* ज़ोए ظ (English jh हिंदी ज़)

ظ	ظـ	ـظـ	ـظ
Stand Alone	End Position	Middle Position	Starting Positoin

NOTE : This is the second ज *'j'* sound (see : जीम *jīm* in Lesson 3.7, ज़े *je* in Lesson 3.16, ज़े *je* in Lesson 3.17, ज़ुआद *juād* in Lesson 3.21 and ज़ोए *joe* in Lesson 3.23)

Examples : ज़ोए *zoe* (ظ) : Urdū name *zoe* ظوے (हिंदी ज़ English *j*)

(i) Letter *'zoe'* in Stand-alone position (ظ) :

(ii) Letter *'zoe'* in Starting position (ظـ) : e.g. **ज़ालम, ज़ालिम *jālam, jālim*** (Cruel)

Right to Left ← म *m* + ल *j* + अ *a* + ज *j* = م + ل + ا + ظ = ـم + لـ + ـا + ظـ = ظالم (***zoe*** ظ **in Starting shape, *alif* is in End position as it does not connect on left side; and for the same reason *lām*** ل **takes Starting position. *mīm*** م **is in End position).**

(iii) Letter *'zoe'* in Middle position (ـظـ) : **e.g. मज़्हर *majhar*** (Place of appearance)

Right to Left ← र *r* + ह *h* + ज़ *jh* + म *m* = ر + ہ + ظ + م = ـر + ـہـ + ـظـ + مـ

+ ظـ + مـ = مظہر (*mīm* is in Starting shape, *zoe* and *chhoṭī he* are in Middle shape and *re* is in End shape). For writing letter छोटी हे *chhoṭī he*, please see Lesson 3.34 or the chart on the back cover.

(iv) Letter *'zoe'* in End position (ـظ) : e.g. हफ़ीज *hafīz* (Protector) Right to Left ← ज *t* + इ *i* + फ़ *f* + ह *h* = ظ + ی + ح + ف = ـظ + ـیـ + ـفـ + حـ = حفیظ (*he* ح is in Starting shape, *fe* ف and *chhoṭī ye* ی are in Middle shape and *zoe* ظ is in End shape).

NOTE : For writing letters छोटी ये *chhoṭī ye* and फे *fe,* please see Lessons 3.37 and 3.26 or the chart on the back cover of the book.

EXERCISE *mashq* (مشق मश्क) 24 :

1. Read the following Urdū words and write them several times :

حفیظ ظالم حظ

2. Write the following words in Urdū :

ख़त *khat* (Letter), पर *par* (Wing), बत्तख़ *battakh* (Duck), तलब *talab* (Addiction)

LESSON 3.24

The 24th letter of the Urdū Alphabet : *ain* ऐन ع (English e, a हिंदी ए, अ)

ع	ع	ـعـ	عـ
Stand Alone	**End Position**	**Middle Position**	**Starting Positoin**

Examples : ऐन *ain* (ع) : Urdū name *ain* عین (हिंदी ए, अ Eng. *e, a*)

(i) Letter *'ain'* in Stand-alone position (ع)

(ii) Letter *'ain'* in Starting position (عـ) : **e.g. अजब *ajab* (Strange) Right to Left ←**

ब *b* + ज *j* + अ *a* = ب + ج + ع = ـب + ـجـ + عـ = عجب

(*ain* ع is in Starting shape, *jīm* ج is in Middle position and *be* ب is in End position).

(iii) Letter *'ain'* in Middle position (ـعـ) : **e.g. तअब *ta-ab* (Struggle, effort, trouble)**

Right to Left ← ब *b* + अ *a* + त *t* = ب + ع + ت = ـب + ـعـ + تـ = تعب **(*te* ت is in Starting shape, *ain* ع is in Middle position and *be* ب is in End position).**

(iv) Letter *'ain'* in End position (ـع) : **e.g. शमुअ *sham-a* (Wax, candle, lamp) Right to**

Left ← अ *a* + म् *m* + श *sh* = ع + م + ش = ـع + ـمـ + شـ = شمع

(*shīn* ش is in Starting shape, *mīm* م is in Middle shape and *ain* ع is in End shape).

EXERCISE *mashq* (مشق मश्क) 25 :

1. Read the following Urdū words and write them several times :

عجب شمع سچ علم

2. Write the following words in Urdū :

अजब *ajab* (Strange), सच *sach* (True), टप टप *ṭap ṭap* (A sound), इल्म *ilm* (Knowledge)

LESSON 3.25

The 25th letter of the Urdū Alphabet : *gain* गैन غ (English gh हिंदी ग़)

غ	ـغ	ـغـ	غـ
Stand Alone	End Position	Middle Position	Starting Positoin

Examples : गैन *gain* (غ) : Urdū name *gain* غین (हिंदी ग़ Eng. *gh*)

(i) Letter *'gain'* in Stand-alone position (غ)

(ii) Letter *'gain'* in Starting position (غ) : e.g. ग़जब *ghajab* (Outrage, oppresion),

Right to Left ← ब *b* + ज *j* + ग़ *gh* = ب + ض + غ = ب + ضـ

+ غـ = غضب (*gain* غ is in Starting shape, *juād* ض is in Middle position

and *be* ب is in End position).

(iii) Letter *'gain'* in Middle position (ـغـ) : e.g. बग़ल *bagal* (Side, edge, arm-pit) Right

to Left ← ल *l* + ग़ *gh* + ब *b* = ل + غ + ب = ل + ـغـ + بـ =

بغل (*be* ب is in Starting shape, *gain* غ is in Middle position and *lām* ل is in

End position).

(iv) Letter *'gain'* in End position (ـغ) : e.g. सराग़, सुराग़ *surāgh* (Sign, hole) Right to

Left ← ग़ *g* + अ *a* + र *r* + स *s* = غ + ا + ر + س = ـغ + ـا + ـر

+ سـ = سراغ (*sīn* س is in Starting shape, *re* ر and *alif* ا *are* in Middle

shape and *gain* غ is in End shape).

EXERCISE *mashq* (مشق मश्क़) 26 :

1. Read the following Urdū words and write them several times :

عجب غضب بغل سراغ شمع

2. Write the following words in Urdū :

ग़ज़ब *ghazab* (Strange), बग़ल *baghal* (Side), अब *ab* (Now), डर *dar* (Fear), सुराग़ *surāgh* (Hole)

LESSON 3.26

The 26th letter of the Urdū Alphabet : *fe* फ़े ف (English f हिंदी फ़)

ف	ـف	ـفـ	فـ
Stand Alone	End Position	Middle Position	Starting Positoin

Examples : फ़े *fe* (ف) : Urdū name *fe* فے (Hindi फ़ English *f*)

(i) Letter *'fe'* in Stand-alone position (ف)

(ii) Letter *'fe'* in Starting position (فـ) : e.g. फ़ज *faj* (Mountain pass), Right to Left

← ज *j* + फ़ *f* = ج + ف = ج + فـ = فج (*fe* ف is in Starting shape and *jīm* ج is in End position).

(iii) Letter *'fe'* in Middle position (ـفـ) : e.g. सफ़ा *safā* (Page) Right to Left ← ह *h* + फ़ *f* + स *s* =

ہ + ف + ض = و + ف + س = صفہ (*suād* ص is in Starting shape, *fe* ف is in Middle position and *chhoti he* ہ is in End position).

(iv) Letter *'fe'* in End position (ـف) : e.g. तफ़ *taf* (Heat, warmth) Right to Left ← फ़ *f* + त *t* = ف + ت = ف + ت = تف (*te* ت is in Starting shape, and *fe* ف is in End shape).

EXERCISE *mashq* (مشق मश्क़) 27 :

1. Read the following Urdū words and write them several times :

فج   رف   طرف   صفحہ

2. Write the following words in Urdū :

तरफ़ *taraf* (Towards, side), बरफ़ *baraf* (Ice), साफ़ *sāf* (Clean)

LESSON 3.27

The 27th letter of the Urdū Alphabet : *qāf* क़ाफ़ ق (English q Hindi क़)

ق	ـق	ـقـ	قـ
Stand Alone	End Position	Middle Position	Starting Positoin

NOTE : This is the first क *'k'* type of sound (see : काफ़ *kāf* Lesson 3.28)

Examples : क़ *q* (ق) : Urdū name *qāf* قاف (हिंदी क़ English *q*)

(i) Letter *'qāf'* in Stand-alone position (ق)

(ii) Letter *'qāf'* in Starting position (قـ) : e.g. क़तल *qatal* (Murder, slaughter), Right

to Left ← ल *l* + त *t* + क़ *q* = ل + ت + ق = ل + تـ + قـ =

قتل (*qāf* ق is in Starting shape, *te* ت is in Middle position, and lām ل is in End position).

(iii) Letter *'qāf'* in Middle position (ـقـ) : e.g. फ़क़त *faqat* (Only) Right to Left ← त *t* + क़ *q* + फ़ *f* = ط + ق + ف = ط + قـ + فـ = فقط (*fe* ف is in Starting shape, *qāf* ق is in Middle position and *toe* ق is in End position).

(iv) Letter *qāf* in End position (ـق) : e.g. सबक़ *sabaq* (Lesson) Right to Left ← क़ *q* + ब *b* + स *s* = ق + ب + س = ق + بـ + سـ = سبق (*sīn* س is in Starting shape, *be* ب is in Middle Shape and *qāf* ق is in End shape).

EXERCISE *mashq* (مشق मश्क़) 28 :

1. Read the following Urdū words and write them several times :

صحہ   فقط   سبق   رف

2. Write the following words in Urdū :

हक़ *haq* (Right, claim), सबक़ *sabaq* (Lesson), फ़रक़ *faraq* (Difference)

URDU LETTERS GROUP 6 (based on Character Shapes)

LESSON 3.28

The 28th letter of the Urdū Alphabet : *kāf* काफ़ ک (English k Hindi क)

ک	ـک	ـکـ	کـ
Stand Alone	End Position	Middle Position	Starting Positoin

NOTE : This is the second क *'k'* type of sound (see : क़ाफ़ *qāf* Lesson 3.27)

REMEMBER : **Letters काफ़ *kāf* (ک) and गाफ़ *gāf* (گ) form the sixth group of letters which can be identified simply by looking at the mark (*nuqte*). Letter काफ़ *kāf* is explained here and गाफ़ *gāf* is explained in the next section.**

Examples : क *k* (ک) : Urdu namē *kāf* کاف (Hindī क English *k*)

(i) Letter *'kāf'* in Stand-alone position (ک)

(ii) Letter *kāf* in Starting position (کـ) : **e.g. कफ़ *kaf* (Palm, hand, paw), Right to Left ← फ़ *f* + क *k* = ف + ک = ف + کـ = کف (*kāf* ک is in**

Starting shape, *fe* ف is in End position).

(iii) Letter *'kāf'* in Middle position (کـ) : e.g. शकर *shakar* (Sugar) Right to Left ← र

r + क *k* + श *sh* = ر + ک + ش = ـر + ـکـ + شـ = شکر (*shīn*

ش is in Starting shape, *kāf* ک is in Middle position and *re* ر is in End position).

(iv) Letter *'kāf'* in End position (ـک) : e.g. एक *aik* (One) Right to Left ← क *k* + इ

i + अ *a* = ک + ی + ا = ـک + یـ + ا = ایک (*alif* ا is in

Starting and Stand alone shape, *chhoti ye* ی is in Middle shape, and *kāf* is in End position).

EXERCISE *mashq* (مشق मश्क) 29 :

1. Read the following Urdū words and write them several times :

سبق بطخ ناک کف شکر کب

2. Write the following words in Urdū :

बतख़ *batakh* (Duck), सबक़ *sabaq* (Lesson), शकर *shakar* (Sugar), शक *shak* (Doubt)

LESSON 3.29

The 29th letter of the Urdū Alphabet : *gāf* गाफ़ گ (English g Hindi ग)

گ ـگ ـگـ گـ

Stand Alone **End Position** **Middle Position** **Starting Positoin**

Examples : ग *g* (گ) : Urdū name *gāf* گاف (हिंदी ग English *g*)

(i) Letter *'gāf'* in Stand-alone position (گ)

(ii) Letter *'kāf'* in Starting position (گـ) : **e.g. गप *gap* (Chatter), Right to Left ← प**

***p* + ग *g* =** پ + گ = ـپ + گـ = گپ (*gāf* گ **is in Starting**

shape and *pe* پ is in End position)

(iii) Letter *'gāf'* in Middle position (ـگـ) : **e.g. शगर *shagar* (Wasp, hornet) Right to**

Left ← र *r* + ग *g* + श *sh* = ر + گ + ش = ـر + ـگـ + شـ =

شگر (***shīn*** ش **is in Starting shape, *gāf*** گ **is in Middle position and *re*** ر **is in End**

position).

(iv) Letter *'gāf'* in End position (ـگ) : e.g. सग *sag* (Dog) Right to Left ← ग *g* + स

s = گ + س = ـگ + سـ = سگ) (*sīn* س is in Starting shape, *gāf*

گ is in End position).

EXERCISE *mashq* (مشق मश्क) 30 :

1. Read the following Urdū words and write them several times :

سگ شگر مگر گرم

2. Write the following words in Urdū :

गरम *garam* (Hot), मगर *magar*(But), शगर *shagar* (Bee), बद *bad* (Bad)

LESSON 3.30

The 30th letter of the Urdū Alphabet : *lām* लाम ل (English l Hindi ल)

ل	ـل	ـلـ	لـ
Stand Alone	End Position	Middle Position	Starting Positoin

REMEMBER : Letters लाम *lām* (ل) and नून *nūn* (ن) and nun gunnah (ں see page 12) form the seventh group of letters which can be identified simply by looking at the dot (*nuqte*).

Examples : ल *l* (ل) : Urdū name *lām* لام (हिंदी ल English *l*)

(i) Letter *'lām'* in Stand-alone position (ل)

(ii) Letter *'lām'* in Starting position (لـ) : e.g. **लब** ***lab*** **(Lip), Right to Left ← ब** ***b*** **+**

ल *l* = ب + ل = ب + لـ = لب (***lām*** ل **is in Starting shape,**

be ب **is in End position)**

(iii) Letter *'lām'* in Middle position (ـلـ) : e.g. **बला** ***balā*** **(Trouble) Right to Left ← अ**

a + ल *l* + ब *b* = ا + ل + ب = ا + ـلـ + بـ = بلا (***be*** ب **is in**

Starting shape and ***lām*** ل **is in Middle position and** ***alif*** **is in End position).**

(iv) Letter *'lām'* in End position (ـل) : e.g. **बगल** ***bagal*** **(Side, edge) Right to Left ←**

ल *l* + ग *g* + ब *b* = ل + غ + ب = ـل + ـغـ + بـ = بغل (***be***

is in Starting shape, ***gain*** غ **is in Middle shape and** ***lām*** ل **is in End position).**

EXERCISE *mashq* (مشق मश्क) **31 :**

1. Read the following Urdū words and write them several times :

بلا بال کل لب بگل

2. Write the following words in Urdū :

बगल *bagal* (Side), मगर *magar* (But), बला *balā* (Misfortune)

LESSON 3.31

The 31st letter of the Urdū Alphabet : *mīm* मीम م (English m Hindi म)

م	ـم	ـمـ	مـ
Stand Alone	**End Position**	**Middle Position**	**Starting Positoin**

Examples : म *m* (م) : Urdū name *mīm* میم (हिंदी म English *m*)

(i) Letter *'mīm'* in Stand-alone position (م)

(ii) Letter *'mīm'* in Starting position (مـ) : e.g. मत *mat* (Don't), Right to Left ← त *t* + म *m* =

ت + م = ـت + مـ = مت (*mīm* م is in Starting shape and *te* ت is in End position)

(iii) Letter *'mīm'* in Middle position (ـمـ) : e.g. कमर *kamar* (Waist) Right to Left ← र *r* + म *m* + क *k* = ر + م + ک = ـر + ـمـ + کـ = کمر (*kāf* ک is in Starting shape, *mīm* م is in Middle position and *re* ر is in End position).

(iv) Letter *'mīm'* in End position (ـم) : e.g. कम *kam* (Less) Right to Left ← म *m* +

क *k* = م + ک = م + ک = کم (*kāf* ک is in Starting shape and *mīm* م is in End position).

EXERCISE *mashq* (مشق मश्क) 32 :

1. Read the following Urdū words and write them several times :

مت ٹماٹر تم کر کم

2. Write the following words in Urdū :

कमल Kamal (A *proper noun; Lotus*), कम *kam* (Less), टमाटर *ṭmāṭar* (Tomato), मत *mat* (Don't)

LESSON 3.32

The 32nd letter of the Urdū Alphabet : *nūn* नून ن (English n Hindi न)

ن	ـن	ـنـ	نـ
Stand Alone	End Position	Middle Position	Starting Positoin

Examples : न *n* (ن) : Urdū name *nūn* نون (हिंदी न English *n*)

(i) Letter *'nūn'* in Stand-alone position (ن)

(ii) Letter *'nūn'* in Starting position (نـ) : e.g. नाम *nām* (Name), Right to Left ← म

m + अ *a* + न *n* = م + ا + ن = م + ـا + نـ = نام (*nūn* ن is in Starting shape, *alif* is in Middle shape and *mīm* م is in Stand alone position)

(iii) Letter *'nūn'* in Middle position (ﻨ) : e.g. जनाब *janāb* (Sir) Right to Left ← ब *b* + अ *a* + न *n* + ज *j* = ب + ا + ن + ج = ﺐ + ﺎ + ﻨ + ﺟ

= جناب (*jīm* is in Starting shape, *nūn and alif* are in Middle position and *be* is in End position).

(iv) Letter *'nūn'* in End position (ﻦ) : e.g. लगन *lagan* (Longing, attachment) Right to Left ← न *n* + ग *g* + ल *l* = ن + گ + ل = ﻦ + ﮔ + ﻟ =

لگن (*lām* ل is in Starting shape, *gāf* گ in Middle shape, *nūn* ن is in End position).

EXERCISE *mashq* (مشق मश्क) 33 :

1. Read the following Urdū words and write them several times :

لگن   جان   جناب   برتن   نام

2. Write the following words in Urdū :

बरतन *bartan* Pot), लगन *lagan* (Affection), लगान *lagān* (Rent), नाम *nām* (Name), जनाब *janāb* (Sir), शराब *sharāb* (Wine); बरतन *bartan* (Pot).

URDU LETTERS GROUP 7 (based on Character Shapes)

LESSON 3.33

The 33rd letter of the Urdū Alphabet :

vāo वाओ و (English V, W Hindi व, उ, औ)

و	ـو	ـو	و
Stand Alone	End Position	Middle Position	Starting Positoin

REMEMBER :

(1) Letter *vāo* वाओ (و) is similar to letter दाल *dāl* (د) in shape, and thus sometimes confusing.

(2) Letter *vāo* वाओ (و) stands for English letters V and W, (Hindi व). It is many times used as Hindī vowels उ, ओ or औ (*u, o, au*) attached to consonants. eg. दुकान (*dukān*,Shop) دکان ; दो (*do*,Two) دو ; सौ (*sau*,Hundred) سو

Examples : व *v* : Urdū name *vāo* واو (हिंदी व English *v, w*)

(i) Letter *'vāo'* in Stand-alone position (و)

(ii) Letter *'vāo'* in Starting position (و) : e.g. वतन *vatan* (Homeland), Right to Left

← न *n* + त *t* + व *v* = ن + ط + و = ن + ط + و = وطن (*vāo* و is in Starting Stand alone shape, therefore, *toe* ط is in Starting shape. *nūn* ن is in End position)

(iii) Letter *'vāo'* in Middle position (ـو) : e.g. जवान *jawān* (Young) Right to Left ← न *n* + अ *a* + व *w* + ज *j* = ن + ا + و + ج = ن + ا + ـو + جـ

= جوان (*jīm* ج is in Starting shape, *vāo* و and *alif* ا are in Middle position and *nūn* ن is in End position).

(iv) Letter *'vāo'* in End position (ـو) : e.g. सौ *sau* (Hundred) Right to Left ← औ *au*, *w* + स *s* =

و + س = ـو + سـ = سو (*sīn* س is in Starting shape and *vāo* و is in End position).

EXERCISE *mashq* (مشق मश्क) 34 :

1. Read the following Urdū words and write them several times :

وطن سو جواب جوان دوا

2. Write the following words in Urdū : : सौ *sau* (Hundred), वादा *vādā* (Promise), दवा *davā* (Medicine), बदन *badan* (body), जवाब *javāb* (Reply)

LESSON 3.34

The 34th letter of the Urdū Alphabet : *chhoṭī he* छोटी है ہ (English h Hindi ह)

ہ	ـہ	ـہـ	ہـ
Stand Alone	**End Position**	**Middle Position**	**Starting Positoin**

This is the second ह *'h'* sound

(see : बड़ी है *baḍī he* 3.9 and दो चश्मी है *do chashmī he* 3.35)

NOTES :

(1) At Starting position, sometimes Letter no. 35 दो चश्मी है is used in place of Letter no. 34 छोटी है.

(2) In Naskh (Arabic) writing, sometimes a special shape called '*Hanging he*' is used, but not in Urdū Nastā'leeq writing.

Examples : *h* ह : Urdū name *chhoṭī he* چھوٹی ہے (हिंदी ह, English *h*)

(i) Letter *'chooṭī he'* in Stand-alone position (ہ)

(ii) Letter *'chooṭī he'* in Starting position (ہـ) : **The inverted *comma* sign is optional.**

e.g. हम *ham* (We), Right to Left ← म *m* + ह *h* = م + ہ = مـ + ﮪ = ہم

ہم (*chhoṭī he* ہ is in Starting Stand alone shape and *mīm* م is in End position)

(iii) Letter *'chooṭī he'* in Middle position (ـﮩـ) : e.g. बहा *bahā* (Price) Right to Left ←

अ *a* + ह *h* + ब *b* = ا + ہ + ب = ـا + ـﮩـ + بـ = بہا (*be* ب is

in Starting shape, *chhoṭī he* ہ is in Middle position and *alif* is in End position).

(iv) Letter *'chooṭī he'* in End position (ـہ) : e.g. तह *tah* (Bottom) Right to Left ← ह *h*

+ त *t* = ہ + ت = ـہ + تـ = تہ (*te* ت is in Starting shape and *chhoṭī he*

ہ is in End position).

EXERCISE *mashq* (مشق मश्क) 35 :

1. Read the following Urdū words and write them several times :

ہم   کہنا   یہ   وہ   تہہ

2. Write the following words in Urdū :

वह *vah* (He, that), यह *yah* (This), तह *tah* (layer), कह *kah* (Say), हम *ham* (We)

The 35th letter : *do chashmī he* दो चश्मी हे ھ (English h Hindi ह)

ھ	ـھ	ـھـ	ھـ
Stand Alone	**End Position**	**Middle Position**	**Starting Positoin**

NOTE : This is the third ह *'h'* sound

(see : छोटी हे *chhoṭī he* 3.34 and बड़ी हे *baḍī he* 3.9)

REMEMBER :

This interesting looking character is very important for writing the Hindī 'Breath Characters' namely : ख *kha,* घ *gha,* छ *chha,* झ *jha,* ठ *ṭha,* ढ *ḍha,* ढ़ *ḍha,* थ *tha,* ध *dha,* फ *pha,* and भ *bha.* See chart given below for actual details.

Examples : ह *h* : Urdū name *do chashmī he* دو چشمی ھے (Hindi ह, English *h*)

(i) Letter *'do chashmī he'* in Stand-alone position (ھ)

(ii) Letter *'do chashmī he'* in Starting position (ھـ) : **e.g. हफ़्तः *haftaḥ* (Week), Right to Left** ← ह *h* + त *t* + फ़ *f* + ह *h* = ہ + ت + ف + ھ = ـہ + تـ + فـ + ھـ = ھفتہ = ھفتہ (*do chashmī he* ھ **is in Starting shape,** *fe*

ـنـ *and te* ـتـ are in Middle shape and *chhoṭī he* ہ is in End shape)

(iii) Letter *'do chashmī he'* in Middle position (ـھـ) : e.g. घर *ghar* (House, home)

Right to Left ← र *r* + घ *gh* = ر + ھ + گ = ـر + ـھـ + گـ = گھر

(*gāf* گـ is in Starting shape, *do chashmī he* ھ is in Middle position and *re* ر is in End position).

(iv) Letter *'do chashmī he'* in End position (ـھ) : e.g. रख *rakh* (Keep!) Right to Left

← ख *kh* + र *r* = ھ + ک + ر = ـھ + ـکـ + ر = رکھ (*re* is in Starting shape, *kāf* is in Middle shape and *do chashmī he* ھ is in End position).

EXERCISE *mashq* (مشق मश्क) 36 :

1. Read the following Urdū words and write them several times :

ہفتے شہد کھا کھانا گھر رکھ

2. Write the following words in Urdū :

रख *rakh* (Keep), खाना *khāna* (Food), घर *ghar* (Home), शहद *shahad* (Honey), हम *ham* (We)

3.36 WRITING HINDI BREATH CHARACTERS IN URDU

हुरूफ़ मुरक्कब حروف مرکب

हिंदी : ख *kha,* घ *gha,* छ *chha,* झ *jha,* ठ *ṭha,* ढ *ḍha,* ढ़ *ḍha,*

थ *tha,* ध *dha,* फ *pha,* भ *bha*

Hindī	Urdū		e.g.
ख	*kha* = *kāf* + *do chashmī he*	ھ + ک = کھ	e.g. رکھ रख ***rakh*** (keep)
घ	*gha* = *gāf* + *do chashmī he*	ھ + گ = گھ	e.g. گھر घर ***ghar*** (home)
छ	*chha* = *che* + *do chashmī he*	ھ + چ = چھ	e.g. چھت छत ***chhat*** (roof)
झ	*jha* = *jīm* + *do chashmī he*	ھ ج + = جھ	e.g. جھٹ झट ***jhaṭ*** (quick)
ठ	*ṭha* = *ṭe* + *do chashmī he*	ھ + ٹ = ٹھ	e.g. لٹھ लठ ***laṭh*** (stick)
ढ	*ḍha* = *ḍāl* + *do chashmī he*	ھ + ڈ = ڈھ	e.g. ڈھب ढब ***ḍhab*** (mode)
ढ़	*ḍha* = *aḍe* + *do chashmī he*	ھ + ڑ = ڑھ	e.g. پڑھ पढ़ ***paḍh*** (read)
थ	*tha* = *te* + *do chashmī he*	ھ + ت = تھ	e.g. رتھ रथ ***rath*** (Chariot)
ध	*dha* = *dāl* + *do chashmī he*	ھ + د = دھ	e.g. دھن धन ***dhan*** (wealth)
फ	*pha* = *pe* + *do chashmī he*	ھ + پ = پھ	e.g. پھل फल ***phal*** (fruit)
भ	*bha* = *be* + *do chashmī he*	ھ + ب = بھ	e.g. بھٹ भट ***bhaṭ*** (warrior)

LESSON 3.36

The 36th letter of the Urdū Alphabet *hamzā* हमज़ा ء (English i Hindi इ)

ء ئ

Stand Alone **As Vowel Seperator**

REMEMBER :

(1) Many times,the Urdū letter *hamzā* is indicated by an elevated sign of two dots connected by a slanted line **over the following letter. e.g. (** ؤ **),(** ئ **)**

(2) Rules for use of *hamzā* are inconsistent.

When *hamzā* is used for producing the sounds of the Hindi vowels इ, ऐ, it is placed above these letters.

(3) At the End of a word, it is written as Stand alone letter.e.g. मा *mā* (Sap, essence, juice, water) ماء

EXAMPLES : Urdu name hamzā हमज़ा ہمزہ (Hindi इ, English *i*)

मा *mā* (Sap, essence, juice, water) ماء **चाय *chāy* (Tea)** چائے

LESSON 3.37

The 37th letter : *chhoṭī ye* छोटी ये ی (English y Hindi य, इ)

ی	ـی	ـیـ	یـ
Stand Alone	End Position	Middle Position	Starting Positoin

NOTE : This is the first य *'y'* type of sound (see : बड़ी ये *baḍī ye* 3.38)

FOUR NOTES :

(1) ***chhoṭī ye*** **is sometimes used as consonant य *y* when comes as initial character, but mostly used as vowel इ or ई *i* or *ī* when it comes after a consonant.**

e.g. (i) या *yā* (alif ا + *hhoṭī ye* ی (یا (ii) की *ki* (*chhoṭī ye* ی + *kāf* ک) کی

(2) In itial position in a sentence, letter इ *i* is written as a slante line (*zer*) drawn under the letter *alif*. e.g. इधर *idhar* (On this side) اِدھر

(3) In itial and Middle positions, *chhoṭī ye* is recognized by the conspicuous two dots under the letter. e.g. ईद *īd* عید *(ain + chhoṭī ye + dāl)*

(4) *chhoṭī ye* is mostly used for Feminine words.

e.g. बेटी *beṭī* (daughter) بیٹی (*be + chhoṭī ye + ṭe + chhoṭī ye*)

Examples : य, इ *y, i* ی : Urdū name *chhoṭī ye* چھوٹی یے (हिंदी य, इ English *v, w*)

(i) Letter *'chhoṭī ye'* in Stand-alone position (ی)

(ii) Letter *'chhoṭī ye'* in Starting position (یـ) : e.g. या *yā* (Or), Right to Left ← अ *a* + य *y* = ا + ی = ـا + یـ = یا (*chhoṭī ye* ی is in itial shape and *alif* is in End position)

(iii) Letter *'chhoṭī ye'* in Middle position (ـیـ) : e.g. तीन *tīn* (Three) Right to Left ← न *n* + ई *ī* + त *t* = ن + ی + ت = ـن + ـیـ + تـ = تین (*te* ت is in Starting shape, *chhoṭī ye* ی is in Middle position and *nūn* ن is in End position).

(iv) Letter *'chhoṭī ye'* in End position (ـی) : e.g. पी *pī* (Drink) Right to Left ← ई *ī* + प *p* = ی + پ = ـی + پـ = پی (*pe* پ is in Starting shape and *chhoṭī ye* ی is in End position).

EXERCISE *mashq* (مشق मश्क) 38 :

1. Read the following Urdū words and write them several times :

پی تین کی کیا یا

2. Write the following words in Urdū :

की *kī* (Did), पी *pī* (Drank), ली *lī* (Took), दी *dī* (Gave), या *yā* (Or), बिन *bin* (Without)

LESSON 3.38

The 38th letter of the Urdū alphabet : ***baḍī ye*** बड़ी ये ے (English e Hindi ए)

ے	ـے	ـیـ	یـ
Stand Alone	End Position	Middle Position	Starting Positoin

This is the first य *'y'* type of sound (see : छोटी ये *chhoṭī ye* 3.37)

NOTES :

TIP 7 : Similar to the ***chhoṭī ye, baḍī ye*** is also used as vowel ए *e* when comes after anothervowel or a consonant. eg. (i) या *yā* (*alif* ا + *chhoṭī ye* ی) یا (ii) सेब *seb* (*be* ب + *badi ye* ے + *sIn* س) سیب (ii) सी *sī* (*sīn* + *chhoṭī ye*) سی (ii) से *se* (*baḍī ye* ے + *sīn* سے (س

TIP 8 : Similar to Letters दाल *dāl* (د), डाल *ḍāl* (ڈ), ज़ाल *jāl* (ذ); रे *re* (ر), अड़े *aḍe* (ڑ), ज़े *zay* (ز), ज्ये *zhe* (ژ) and *vāo* वाओ (و), letter *baḍī ye* (ے) also does not connect to the letter on its left side.

e.g. बेकस *bekas* بےکس (*sīn* س + *kāf* ک + *baḍī ye* ے + *be* ب)

TIP 9 : In Middle positions, sometimes *chhoṭī ye* is used in place of the *baḍī ye.* and then it is easily recognized by the conspicuous two dots under the letter.

e.g. (1) बेकस *bekas* بےکس (*sīn* س + *kāf* ک + *baḍī ye* ے + *be* ب) (2) एक *ek (aik)* ایک (*kāf* ک + *chhoṭī ye* ی + *alif* ا)

TIP 10 : ***baḍī ye*** **is mostly used for Masculine words and chhoṭī ye for Feminine words.**

Examples : य, इ *y, i* ے : Urdū name *baḍī ye* بڑی یے (हिंदी ए English *e*)

(i) Letter *'baḍī ye'* in Stand-alone position (ے)

(ii) Letter *'baḍī ye'* in Starting position (یـ) : **In Starting position, *alif* and *chhoṭī ye* is used in place of *baḍī ye*. .e.g. एबक *ebak* (Slave), Right to Left ← क *k* + ब *b* + ए *e* + अ *a* =** ک + ب + ی + ا = ک + بـ + یـ + ا = ایبک

(*alif* ا and *chhoṭī ye* ی are in Initial shape, *be* ب is in Middle shape and *kāf* ک is in End position)

(iii) Letter *'baḍī ye'* in Middle position (ے) : **e.g. बेकुव्वत *bequvat* (Unfir) Right to Left ← त *t* + व *v* + क *k* + ए *e* + ब *b* =** ت + و + ق + ے + ب = ت + و + ک + یـ + بـ = بےقوت **(*be* ب is in Starting shape, *baḍī ye* ے and *qāf* ق and vāo و are in Middle position and *te* ت is in stand alone position).**

(iv) Letter *'baḍī ye'* in End position (ے) : **e.g. ले *le* (Take!) Right to Left ← ए *e* + ल *l* =** ے + ل = ے + لـ = لے **(*lām* ل is in Starting shape and *baḍī ye* ے is in End position).**

EXERCISE *mashq* (مشق मश्क) 39 :

1. Read the following Urdū words and write them several times :

سب ایک میرا اک لے لےکس

2. Write the following words in Urdū :

ले *le* (Take), दे *de* (Give), मेरा *merā* (My), बेकस *bekas* (Sad), या *yā* (Or)

LESSON 3.39

The 39th letter of the Urdū alphabet :

nūnehgunnah नूने गुन्ना (English *an* Hindi अँ)

ں ں

Stand Alone End Position

Also called नून गुन्ना Nūn gunnā, it acts almost same as the signs for Hindi vowels आँ or एँ (चंद्रबिंदी ँ मात्रा) at the end of a word. **Remember :**

(i) This नून गुन्ना Nūne gunnaḥ character comes only at the end of a word.

(ii) Its shape is almost same as letter नून *nūn*, but without the dot.

EXAMPLES :

e.g. माँ *mā̃* ماں क्यों *kyõ* کیوں कहाँ *kahā̃* کہاں

वहाँ *vahā̃* وہاں मैं *maĩ* میں

ESSON 3.40

Study of sentences made up of multiple-letter-words.

दो से सात तक हरफ़ों वाले लफ़्ज़ों के जुमलों की मश्क़

دو سے سات تک حرفوں والے لفظوں کے جملوں کی مشق

EXAMPLES : मिसाल مثال

A. Words of Two Letters : दो हरफ़ी लफ़्ज़ دو حرفی لفظ

1. آگ āg आग (Fire)

2. کب؟ kab कब (When?)

3. بم bam बम (Bomb)

4. بم bam बम (Bomb)

TWO IMPORTANT NOTES :

(1) If *alif* (ا) or Lam (ل) comes after *kāf* (ک), the compound letter becomes like

کا kā का (Of), کل kal कल (Yesterday, Tomorrow)

(2) If Alif (ا) comes after Lam (ل), the compound letter becomes like this :

لا or لا lā ला (Please bring), لابھ lābh लाभ (Benefit)

(2) Study of sentences of TWO-LETTERS words : دو حرفی لفظوں کی مشق

1. Bring two letters. *do khat lā.* दो खत ला دو خط لا

2. Don't count days. *din mat gin* दिन मत गिन دن مت گن

3. Drink juice. *ras pī le.* रस पी ले رس پی لے

(3) Words of THREE LETTERS : तीन हरफ़ी लफ़्ज़ تین حرفی لفظ

1. رات *rāt* रात (Night)
2. باپ *bāp* बाप (Father)
3. بام bam बम (Bomb)
4. قلم kalam क़लम (Pen)

Study of sentences of three-letters words : تین حرفی لفظوں کی مشق

1. Tea is hot. *chāy garam hai.* चाय गरम है گرم ہے چائے
2. Take three steps. *tīn qadam chalo* तीन क़दम चलो. تین قدم چلو
3. Say it four times. *Chār bār bol.* चार बार बोल چار بار بول

(4) Words of FOUR LETTERS : चार हरफ़ी लफ़्ज़ چار حرفی لفظ

1. کھانا *khānā* खाना (Food)
2. لڑکا *laḍka* लड़का (Boy)
3. لڑکی laḍkī लड़की (Girl)
4. کپڑا kapḍā कपड़ा (Cloth)

Study of sentences of four-letters words : چار حرفی لفظوں کی مشق

1. Ramesh is my partner. *Ramesh mera sāthī hai.* रमेश मेरा साथी है।
2. رمیش میرا ساتھی ہے *Mere kapḍe safed haĩ.* मेरे कपड़े सफ़ेद हैं।
3. میٹھے چاول لاؤ Bring the sweet rice. *Mīṭhe chāval lāo.* मीठे चावल लाओ।

(5) Words of FIVE LETTERS : पाँच हरफ़ी लफ़्ज़ پانچ حرفی لفظ

1. اکیلا *akelā* अकेला (Single)

2. بیمار *bīmār* बीमार (Sick)

3. زندگی zindagi ज़िंदगी (Life)

4. مبارک mubārak मुबारक (Congratulations)

Study of sentences of five-letters words : پانچ حرفی لفظوں کی مشق

1. Our father is ill. *hamāre pitājī bīmār hain.* हमारे पिताजी बीमार हैं। ہمارے پتاجی بیمار ہیں
2. Rabbit is an animal. *Kahargosh jānvar hai.* ख़रगोश जानवर है। خرگوش جانور ہے
3. Mumtaz is unaware. *Mumtāz bekhabar hai.* मुमताज़ बेख़बर है। ممتاز بے خبر ہے

(6) Words of SIX LETTERS : छह हरफ़ी लफ़्ज छ حرفی لفظ

1. مہربان *meharbān* मेहरबान (Mercyful)

2. انتظار *intizār* इन्तिज़ार (Wait)

3. ترکاری tarkārī तरकारी (Vegetable)

4. دروازہ darvā!zā दरवाज़ा (Door)

Study of sentences of six-letters words : چھ حرفی لفظوں کی مشق

1. Preparation for the examination. *imtehan kā intizām.* इम्तिहान का इन्तिज़ाम।

امتحاں کا انتظام

2. Please don't flatter! *Khushāmad mat kījiye.* ख़ुशामद मत कीजिये।

خوشامد مت کیجے

3. Shivram is a wicked person. *Shivrām badmāsh hai.* शिवराम बदमाश है।

شیورام بدمعاش ہے

(7) Words of SEVEN LETTERS : सात हरफ़ी लफ़्ज़ سات حرفی لفظ

1. کارخانہ *kārkhānā* कारख़ाना (Factory)

2. زمیندار *zamīndār* ज़मींदार (Landlord)

3. دیوانگی dīvānagī दीवानगी (Craze)

4. انگریزی angrezī अंग्रेज़ी (English)

5. امیدوار ummīdvār. उम्मीदवार (Candidate, applicant, hopeful)

6. انسانیت insāniyat इनसानियत (Humanity)

7. بدقسمتی badkismatī बदक़िसमती (Misfortune)

Study of sentences of seven-letters words : سات حرفی لفظوں کی مشق

1. Get the pictures prepared. *tasvīrẽ banavāiye.* तसवीरें बनवाइये। تصویریں بنوائیے

2. A rich farmer. *daulatmand kashtakār.* दौलतमन्द काश्तकार।

دولتمند کاشتکار

3. Oil refinary. *Petroleum ka kārkhānā.* पेट्रोलियम का कारख़ाना।

پٹرولیم کا کارخانہ

LESSON 4

WRITING HINDI AND ENGLISH VOWELS IN URDU

हिंदी और अंग्रेज़ी स्वरों को उर्दू में लिखना ।

اردو میں ہندی اور انگریزی سر لکھنا

(1) अ (a) : ا

For producing the sound of Short vowel 'a', as the first 'A' in the English word 'America' अमेरीका, or Hindi word अब *ab,* please see Urdū letter *alif* in Section 3.1 above. eg. अमरीका *amrikā* (America) امریکہ

(2) आ (ā, aa) : آ

(i) To write the Long vowel 'ā' (आ) sound at the begining of a word, like आ *ā* in the word आग *āg* (Fire), write the letter *alif* and put a 'tilde' like sign (˜) above to make it look like آ e.g. आग *āg* (Fire) آگ

(ii) The Long 'ā' sound within or at the end of the word : like आ *ā* in the word माता *mātā* (Mother) ماتا

(3) इ (i) : ا or یا

(i) To write the sound of the Short vowel 'i' (इ), like इ *i* in word रिहा *rihā,* please see Urdū letter *chhoṭī ye* in Section 3.37. e.g. रिहा *rihā* (Free) رہا

(ii) Initial letter, इ *i* is written by adding a diacritical 'French aigue' like subscript 'zer' sign (see the next section). e.g. इतना *itnā* اتنا

(4) ई (ī) : ای

(i) To write the Long vowel 'ī' (ई) sound at the begining of a word, like word ईद *īd*, write the diacritical subscript 'zer' sign below letter *alif,* and then write letter *chhoṭī ye* next to it. e.g. ईद *īd* (a featival) عید

(ii) The Long 'ī' sound within or at the end of the word : like the word नीली *nīlī*, normally the letter *chhoṭī ye* is used. e.g. नीली *nīlī* (Blue) نیلی

(5) उ (u) : ا or و

(i) The Short vowel उ *u* as in English word 'put' or Hindi word दुकान *dukān* is written by diacritical superscript 'pesh' sign (see next lesson) above the consonant to which उ *u* is attached. e.g. दुकान *dukān*(shop) دکان

(ii) Initial letter, उ *u* in a word is written by adding diacritical superscript 'pesh' above letter *alif.* e.g. उतना *utnā* اتنا

(6) ऊ (ū) : او

(i) The Initial Long vowel ऊ *ū* as in Hindi word ऊपर *ūpar* is written by adding 'pesh' above letter *alif* and then writing letter *vāo.* e.g. ऊपर *ūpar*(Above) اوپر

(ii) Within or at the end of a word the letter, उ *u* is indicated by writing superscript 'pesh' above the consonant followed by letter *vāo.* e.g. दूध *dūdh* دودھ उर्दू *urdū* اردو

(7) ए (e) : ے

(i) The Initial vowel sound ए, *ai (or ay)* as in Hindi word एक (अइक) *e, or i (ai, i)* is shown by writing *alif* and *baḍī ye.* e.g. एक *ek* (One) ایک

(ii) Within a word the letter, ए *e* is written as *baḍī ye* in Middle shape which is same as *chhoṭī ye* in the Middle shape. e.g. मेरी *merī* (My) میری (ii) At the End of a word, the letter ए *e* is written by adding 'zabar' mark over the consonant, followed by End-shape of *baḍī ye.* e.g. मेरे *mere* (My)

(8) ऐ (ai) : اے

(i) The Initial vowel sound ऐ *ai* as in Hindī word ऐनक *ainak* is written by writing *ain* followed by letter *baḍī ye in* Middle shape. e.g. ऐनक *ainak* (Eye glasses) عینک

(ii) In the Middle or at the End of a word, the letter ऐ *ai* is indicated by writing *baḍī ye* in Middle or End shape. e.g. पैसा *paisā* (Money) Naskh है *hai* (Is) ہے

(9) ओ (o) : او or و

(i) The Initial vowel sound ओ *o* as in English word 'open' or Hindi word ओम् *om* is written with *alif* followed by letter *vāo.* e.g. ओम् *om* (a Symbol) اوم

(ii) Within or at the End of a word, the letter, ओ *o* is represented by letter *vāo.* e.g. तोता *totā* (Parrot) طوطا Naskh बोलो *bolo* (Speak!) بولو

(10) औ (au) : او

(i) The Initial vowel sound औ *au* (as in English word 'caught' or Hindi word और *aur*) is written as *alif with 'zabar' mark,* followed by letter *vāo.* e.g. और *aur* (And) اور

(ii) Within or at the End of a word, the letter, औ *au* is indicated by writing Middle or End shape of letter *vāo and the 'zabar'* mark on the preceeding consonant. e.g. मौसम *mausam* (Season) موسم

LESSON 5

URDU DIACRITICAL ACCENT MARKS

मात्राएं (ए'राब) اعراب

(1) Zabar ज़बर زبر : e.g. ا ب پ ...etc.

اَ

'Zabar' is always written as SUPERSCRIPT (above). Its shape is like French 'acute accent.' Appearing initially, Zabar should be placed over letter *alif.* It imparts a plain sound (like अ *a*) to the consonant below it. e.g. ا = (अ + अ, *a + a*), ب = (ब् + अ, *b + a*) پ = (प् + अ, *p + a*)

(2) Zer ज़ेर زیر : e.g. پ ب ا ...etc.

اِ

'Zer' is always written as SUBSCRIPT (bolow). Its shape is like French 'accent aigue.'

It adds a sound of इ *i* to the consonant above it.

Appearing initially, Zer should be placed under letter *alif.*

e.g. ا = इ *i*, = बि *bi*, (ब् + इ, *b + i*), = पि *pi*, (प् + इ, *p + i*)

(3) Pesh पेश پیش : e.g. پ ب ا ...etc.

اُ

'Pesh' is always written as SUPERSCRIPT. Its shape is like English 'comma.'

It adds a sound of उ *u* to the consonant below it.

Appearing initially, Pesh should be placed over letter *alif.*

e.g. ا = उ *u*, ب = बु *bu*, (ब् + उ, *b + u*), پ = पु *pi*, (प् + उ, *p + u*)

(4) Mad मद مد : e.g. آ

آ

'Mad' is always written as SUPERSCRIPT. Its shape is like Spanish 'tilde.'

It gives a sound of आ *ā* to the letter *alif.*

'mad' should be placed over letter *alif.* e.g. آپ = आप *āp* (You).

(5) Tashdīd तश्दीद تشدید : e.g. سّ ٹّ تّ پّ بّ ...etc.

w

'Tashdīd' is always written as SUPERSCRIPT. Its shape is like English 'w'

It comes within the substantive words on any consonant other than the initial letter. It duplicates the sound of the letter below it.

Tashdid is not used in verbs, The double consonants in verbs are written fully.

दिल्ली *dillī* دلّی ,دیلی دلی अब्बा *abbā* ا□ب ابا , बच्चा *bacchā* ب□چ , कुत्ता

kuttā ا□کت کتا , बिल्ली *billī* بلی, अम्मा *ammā* اما

(6) Jazma जज़्म جزم (Naskh) : ^

^

'Jazma' is always written as SUPERSCRIPT. Its shape is like French 'circonflex.'

The consonant below the 'circonflex' *Jazma* is a half letter, i.e. the consonant does not have any vowel added to it. In Hindi (and Sanskrit) it is called हलन्त *halant* (्). This occurs when two (or more) consonants come in a row, the last consonant is full (it has a vowel added) and the first consonant is (or rest of the consonants are) half (no vowel added). It will not appear initially.

e.g. दोस्त *dost* (Friend) دوس^ت

(7) Nūnegunnaḥ नूनेगुन्नह् نون غنہ : ں

ں

Also called नून गुन्ना Nūn gunnā, it acts almost same as the signs for Hindi vowels आँ or एँ (चंद्रबिंदी ँ मात्रा) at the end of a word. This नून गुन्ना Nūne gunnaḥ character comes at the end of a word. Its shape is almost same as letter नून *nūn,* but without the dot. *e.g.* माँ *mā̃* ماں

क्यों *kyõ* کیوں ، कहाँ *kahā̃* کہاں , वहाँ *vahā̃* وہاں , मैं *maĩ* میں

Commonly, in Urdū writings, most of these accent marks are ignored, may be as a style.

(A) CHART OF HINDI / ENGLISH / URDU CONSONANTS + VOWELS

अ	आ *ā*	इ *i*	उ *u*	ए *e*	ऐ *ai*	ओ *o*	औ *au*
	ा	ि	ु	े	ै	ो	ौ
क (k) ک	کا	کی	ک	کے	کی	کو	کو
क़ (q) ق	قا	قی	ق	قے	قی	قو	قو
ख (kh) کھ	کھا	کھی	کھ	کھے	کھی	کھو	کھو
ख़ (kh) خ	خا	خی	ح	خے	حی	خو	حو
ग (g) گ	گا	گی	گ	گے	گ	گو	گو
घ (gh) گھ	گھا	گھی	گھ	گھے	گھی	گھو	گھو
च (ch) چ	چا	چی	ح	چے	حی	چو	حو
छ (chh) چھ	چھا	چھی	چھ	چھے	حھی	چھو	حھو
ज (j) ج	جا	جی	ح	جے	حی	جو	حو
ज़ (z) د	دا	دی	د	دے	دی	دو	دو
ज़ (jh) ر	را	ری	ر	رے	ری	رو	رو
ज़्य (zh) ر	را	ری	ر	رے	ری	رو	رو
ज़ (xj) ص	ضا	ضی	ص	ضے	صی	ضو	صو
ज़ (jh) ط	طا	ظی	ط	طے	طی	ظو	طو
झ (jh) جھ	جھا	جھی	جھ	جھے	حھی	جھو	حھو
ट (ṭ) ٮ	ٮا	ٹی	ٮ	ٹے	ٮ	ٹو	ٮو
ठ (ṭh) ٹھ	ٹھا	ٹھی	ٹھ	ٹھے	ٮھی	ٹھو	ٮھو
ड (ḍ) د	دا	دی	د	دے	دی	دو	دو
ड़ (ḍ) ر	را	ری	ر	رے	ری	رو	رو

ढ (ḍh) ڈھ	ڈھا	ڈھی	ڈھ	ڈھے	ڈھی	ڈھو	ڈھو
ढ़ (ḍh) رھ	رھا	رھی	رھ	رھے	رھی	رھو	رھو
त (t) ت	تا	تی	ت	تے	تی	تو	تو
थ (th) تھ	تھا	تھی	تھ	تھے	تھی	تھو	تھو
द (d) د	دا	دی	د	دے	دی	دو	دو
ध (dh) دھ	دھا	دھی	دھ	دھے	دھی	دھو	دھو
न (n) ن	نا	نی	ن	نے	نی	نو	نو
प (p) پ	پا	پی	پ	پے	پی	پو	پو
फ (ph) پھ	پھا	پھی	پھ	پھے	پھی	پھو	پھو
फ़ (f, ph) ف	فا	فی	ف	فے	فی	فو	فو
ब (b) ب	با	بی	ب	بے	بی	بو	بو
भ (bh) بھ	بھا	بھی	بھ	بھے	بھی	بھو	بھو
म (m) م	ما	می	م	مے	می	مو	مو
य (y) ی	یا			یے		یو	
र (r) ر	را	ری	ر	رے	ری	رو	رو
ल (l) ل	لا	لی	ل	لے	لی	لو	لو
व (w) و	وا	وی	و	وے	وی	وو	وو
श (sh) ش	شا	شی	ش	شے	شی	شو	شو
स (s) ث	ثا	ثی	ث	ثے	ثی	ثو	ثو
स (s) س	سا	سی	س	سے	سی	سو	سو
स (s) ص	صا	صی	ص	صے	صی	صو	صو
ह (h) ح	حا	حی	ح	حے	حی	حو	حو

A PRELIMINARY VOCABULARY

OF KEY URDU WORDS

READ the Urdū words and WRITE them.
Understand and remember as many as possible.

1. I मैं *mai̐* میں
2. Is है *hai* ہے
3. I am मैं हूँ *mai̐ hū̐* میں ہوں
4. We हम *ham* ہم
5. You आप *āp* آپ
6. You are तुम हो *tum ho* تم ہو
7. He-She वह, वो *vah, vo* وہ
8. To me मुझे *muzay* مجھے
9. To us हमें *hame̐* مجه سے
10. To him उसको *us ko* اس کو
11. I मैंने *mai̐ne* میں نے
12. You आपने *āp ne* آپ نے
13. You तुमने *tum ne* تم نے
14. From you तुझसे *tujh se* تجھ سے
15. From Him-her उससे *us se* اس سے
16. For me मेरे लिये *mere liye* میرے لئے
17. For you आपके लिये *āpke liye* آپکے لئے

Am हूँ *hū̐* ہوں

Are हैं *hai̐* ہیں

This, it यह, ये *yah, ye* یہ

We are हम हैं *ham hai̐* ہم ہیں

You तुम *tum* تم

You are तू है *tū hai* تو ہے

They वह *vah* وہ

From me मुझसे *mujh se* مجھ سے

To you आपको *āp ko* آپکو

To them उनको *un ko* ان کو

He-She उसने *us ne* اس نے

You तूने *tū ne* تو نے

From you आपसे *āp se* آپ سے

From you तुमसे *tum se* تم سے

From them उनसे *un se* ان سے

18. For us हमारे लिये *hamāre liye* ہمارے لئے

19. For them उनके लिये *unke liye* ان کے لئے

20. My मेरा *merā* میرا — My मेरी *merī* میری

21. My मेरे *mere* تم سے — Our हमारा *hamārā* ہمارا

22. Our हमारी *hamārī* ہماری — Our हमारे *hamāre* ہمارے

23. Your आपका *āp kā* آپ کا — Your आपकी *āp kī* آپکی

24. Your आपके *āp ke* آپکے — In me मुझमें *mujh mẽ* مجھ میں

25. In you तुझमें *tujh mẽ* تجھ میں — In you आपमें *āp mẽ* آپ میں

26. In that उसमें *us mẽ* اس میں — In them उनमें *un mẽ* ان مں

27. On me मुझ पर *mujh par* مجھ پر — On you तुम पर *tum par* تم پر

28. On you तुझ पर *tujh par* تجھ پر — On you आप पर *āp par* آپ پر

29. On that उस पर *us par* اس پر — On this इस पर *is par* اس پر

30. On them उन पर *un par* ان پر — Was था *thā* تھا

31. Was थी *thī* تھی — Were थे *the* تھے

32. What क्या *kyā* کیا — How? कैसे کیسے

33. Ok ठीक *ṭhīk* ٹھیک — Who कौन *kaun* کون

34. Sir! जनाब *janāb* جناب — Name नाम *nām* نام

LESSON 6

THE URDU NUMERALS

उर्दू अदद اردو عدد

0 sifr	• सिफ्र صفر		
1 ek	एक	🕮	One book. ***ek kitāb*** एक किताब। ایک کتاب
2 do	दो	🕮 🕮	Two books. ***dok kitābẽ*** دو کتابیں
3 tīn	तीन	🕮 🕮 🕮	Three books ***tīn kitābẽ*** تین کتابیں
4 chār	चार	🕮 🕮 🕮 🕮	
5 pāñch	पाँच	🕮 🕮 🕮 🕮 🕮	
6 chhah	छह	🕮 🕮 🕮 🕮 🕮 🕮	
7 sāt	सात	🕮 🕮 🕮 🕮 🕮 🕮 🕮	
8 āṭh	आठ	🕮 🕮 🕮 🕮 🕮 🕮 🕮 🕮	
9 nau	नौ	🕮 🕮 🕮 🕮 🕮 🕮 🕮 🕮 🕮	
10 das	दस	🕮 🕮 🕮 🕮 🕮 🕮 🕮 🕮 🕮 🕮	

EXERCISE 39 : Mashq (مشق मश्क) :

(1) Read the numbers in Urdū :

1 7 9 4 0 3 2 8 5 6

(2) Read the following Urdu numerals :

(3) Read and Write the following Urdū numerals :

چار، سات، دو، ایک، آٹھ، دس، نو، پانچ، چھ،

COUNTING FROM ELEVEN TO ONE HUNDRED

Each Urdu Numeral is written Left to Right, like English

English		Transliteration	Hindī	Nastā'leeq
11		*gyārah*	ग्यारह	گیارہ
12		*bārah*	बारह	بارہ
13		*terah*	तेरह	تیرہ
14		*chaudah*	चौदह	چودہ
15		*pandrah*	पंद्रह	پندرہ
16		*solah*	सोलह	سولہ
17		*satrah*	सत्रह	سترہ
18		*aṭhārah*	अठारह	اٹھارہ
19		*unnīs*	उन्नीस	انیس
20		*bīs*	बीस	بیس
21		*ikkīs*	इक्कीस	اکیس
22		*bāīs*	बाईस	بائیس
23		*teīs*	तेईस	تئیس

24		*chaubīs*	चौबीस	چوبیس
25		*pachchīs*	पच्चीस	پچیس
26		*chhabbīs*	छब्बीस	چھبیس
27		*sattāīs*	सत्ताईस	ستائیس
28		*aṭṭhāīs*	अट्ठाईस	اٹھائیس
29		*unatīs*	उनतीस	انتیس
30		*tīs*	तीस	تیس
31		*ikatīs*	इकतीस	اکتیس
32		*battīs*	बत्तीस	بتیس
33		*taĩtīs*	तैंतीस	تینتیس
34		*chaũtīs*	चौंतीस	چونتیس
35		*paĩtīs*	पैंतीस	پینتیس
36		*chhattīs*	छत्तीस	چھتیس
37		*saintīs*	सैंतीस	سینتیس
38		*aṭhattīs*	अठत्तीस	اٹھتیس
39		*untālīs*	उनतालीस	انتالیس
40		*chālīs*	चालीस	چالیس
41		*iktālīs*	इकतालीस	اکتالیس
42		*bayālīs*	बयालीस	بیالیس
43		*taiṅtālīs*	तैंतालीस	تینتالیس
44		*chauvālīs*	चौवालीस	چوالیس
45		*paĩtālīs*	पैंतालीस	پینتالیس

46		*chhiyālīs*	छियालीस	چھیالیس
47		*saiṅtālīs*	सैंतालीस	حالیس سات
48		*aḍatālīs*	अड़तालीस	آر مالیس
49		*unachās*	उनचास	انچاس
50		*pachās*	पचास	پچاس
51		*ikyāvan*	इक्यावन	اکیاون
52		*bāvan*	बावन	باون
53		*tirpan*	तिरपन	ترپن
54		*chauwan*	चौवन	بحاس حار
55		*pachapan*	पचपन	پچپن
56		*chhappan*	छप्पन	چھپن
57		*sattāvan*	सत्तावन	ستاون
58		*aṭṭhāvan*	अट्ठावन	بحاس آٹھ
59		*unasaṭh*	उनसठ	انسٹھ
60		*sāṭh*	साठ	ساٹھ
61		*ikasaṭh*	इकसठ	ساٹھ ایک
62		*bāsaṭh*	बासठ	باسٹھ
63		*tresaṭh*	त्रेसठ	تریسٹھ
64		*chauṅsaṭh*	चौंसठ	ساٹھ حار
65		*paiṅsaṭh*	पैंसठ	پینسٹھ
66		*chhiyāsaṭh*	छियासठ	چھیاسٹھ
67		*saḍasaṭh*	सड़सठ	سڑسٹھ

68		*aḍasath*	अड़सठ	ارسٹھ
69		*unahattar*	उनहत्तर	انہتر
70		*sattar*	सत्तर	ستر
71		*ikahattar*	इकहत्तर	اکہتر
72		*bahattar*	बहत्तर	بہتر
73		*tihattar*	तिहत्तर	تہتر
74		*chauhattar*	चौहत्तर	چوہتر
75		*pachahattar*	पचहत्तर	پچہتر
76		*chhihattar*	छिहत्तर	چھہتر
77		*satahattar*	सतहत्तर	ستہتر
78		*aṭhahattar*	अठहत्तर	اٹھہتر
79		*unyāsī*	उनासी	اناسی
80		*assī*	अस्सी	اسّی
81		*ikyāsī*	इक्यासी	ای اک
82		*bayāsī*	बयासी	بیاسی
83		*tirāsī*	तिरासी	تیراسی
84		*chaurāsī*	चौरासी	چوراسی
85		*pachāsī*	पचासी	پچاسی
86		*chhiyāsī*	छियासी	چھیاسی
87		*sattāsī*	सत्तासी	ستاسی
88		*aṭṭhāsī*	अट्ठासी	اٹھاسی
89		*nāvāsī*	नवासी	نواسی

English		Transliteration	Hindī	Nastā'leeq
90		*nabbe*	नब्बे	نوے
91		*ikyānabe*	इक्यानबे	اکیانوے
92		*bānabe*	बानबे	بانوے
93		*tirānabe*	तिरानबे	ترانوے
94		*chaurānabe*	चौरानबे	لوے حار
95		*pañchānabe*	पचानबे	پچانوے
96		*chhiyānabe*	छियानबे	لوے حھ
97		*sattānabe*	सत्तानबे	ستانوے
98		*aṭṭhānabe*	अट्ठानबे	اٹھانوے
99		*ninyānabe*	निन्यानबे	لوے لو
100		*sau*	सौ	سو

URDU NUMERALS

	0	1	2	3	4	5	6	7	8	9
0	۰	۱	۲	۳	۴	۵	۶	۷	۸	۹
1	۱۰	۱۱	۱۲	۱۳	۱۴	۱۵	۱۶	۱۷	۱۸	۱۹
2	۲۰	۲۱	۲۲	۲۳	۲۴	۲۵	۲۶	۲۷	۲۸	۲۹
3	۳۰	۳۱	۳۲	۳۳	۳۴	۳۵	۳۶	۳۷	۳۸	۳۹
4	۴۰	۴۱	۴۲	۴۳	۴۴	۴۵	۴۶	۴۷	۴۸	۴۹
5	۵۰	۵۱	۵۲	۵۳	۵۴	۵۵	۵۶	۵۷	۵۸	۵۹
6	۶۰	۶۱	۶۲	۶۳	۶۴	۶۵	۶۶	۶۷	۶۸	۶۹
7	۷۰	۷۱	۷۲	۷۳	۷۴	۷۵	۷۶	۷۷	۷۸	۷۹
8	۸۰	۸۱	۸۲	۸۳	۸۴	۸۵	۸۶	۸۷	۸۸	۸۹
9	۹۰	۹۱	۹۲	۹۳	۹۴	۹۵	۹۶	۹۷	۹۸	۹۹

7.1 MAKING YOUR OWN URDU SENTENCES
अपने आप उर्दू जुमले बनाने की मश्क।

اپنے آپ اردو جملے بنانے کی مشق

1 MAKING SIMPLE SENTENCES - **about a** 'Present' event, **with** 'IS' (***hai*** **है**)

NOTE : The ँ sign is a nasal tone added to the vowel under that ँ sign.

English	Hindi	Urdu	English	Hindi	Urdu
I	मैं *(maĩ)*	میں	am	हूँ *(hũ)*	ہوں
You	आप *(āp)*	آپ	are	हैं *(haĩ)*	ہیں
He, she, that	वह *(vah)*	وہ	is	है *(hai)*	ہے
This, it	यह *(yah)*	یہ	They	वह *(vah)*	وہ
My	मेरा *(merā)*	میرا	your	आपका *(āp-kā)*	آپکا
Our	हमारा *(hamārā)*	ہمارا	His/her	उसका *(us-kā)*	اس کا

نقشہ TABLE 1 : Speaking Present Events

Subject		am	is	are
I	मैं *maĩ* میں	हूँ *(hũ)* ہوں		
He, that	वह *vah* وہ		है *(hai)* ہے	
She, that	वह *vah* وہ		है *(hai)* ہے	
We	हम *ham* ہم			हैं *(haĩ)* ہیں
You	आप *āp* آپ			हैं *(haĩ)* ہیں
You	तुम *tum* تم			हो *(ho)* ہو
You	तू *tū* تو			हैं *(haĩ)* ہیں
They	वह *vah* وے			हैं *(haĩ)* ہیں
These	यह *yah* یہ			हैं *(haĩ)* ہیں

NOTE : The above table shows that :

(i) A Present Event is shown by suffix hū̃, hai or haĩ हूँ, है, हैं ہوں , ہے , ہیں

Masuline

I am a boy	मैं लड़का हूँ	maĩ laḍkā hū̃	میں لڑکا ہوں
You are a boy	तू लड़का है	tū laḍkā hai	تو لڑکا ہے
He is a boy	वह लड़का है	vah laḍkā hai	وہ لڑکا ہے
This is a boy	यह लड़का है	yah laḍkā hai	یہ لڑکا ہے

Feminine

I am a girl	मैं लड़की हूँ	maĩ laḍkī hū̃	میں لڑکی ہوں
You are a girl	तू लड़की है	tū laḍkī hai	تو لڑکی ہے
She is a girl	वह लड़की है	vah laḍkī hai	وہ لڑکی ہے
This is a girl	यह लड़की है	yah laḍkī hai	یہ لڑکی ہے

<u>NOTE</u>

<u>BECAUSE URDU IS A DAUGHTER OF HINDI, WITH HINDI GRAMMAR 100% INTACT, HINDI SENTENCES WRITTEN IN URDU SCRIPT ARE URDU SENTENCES.</u>

<u>Like in Hindi, popular and difficult English words</u> may also be used in Urdu sentences **<u>as if they were Urdu words.</u>** See the following exercise for examples.

EXERCISE *mashq* (مشق मश्क) 40 :

Translate the English sentences into Urdu (Answers are given for your help)

1. I am a man. *maĩ ādamī hū̃.* मैं आदमी हूँ। میں آدمی ہوں۔

2. I am a woman. *maĩ aurat hū̃.* मैं औरत हूँ। میں عورت ہوں۔

3. I am a Cashier. *maĩ cashier hū̃.* मैं *cashier* हूँ। میں cashier ہوں۔

4. I am a Judge. *maĩ judge hū̃.* मैं जज हूँ। میں جج ہوں۔

5. I am a Surgeon. *maĩ surgeon hũ.* मैं surgeon हूँ। میں سرجن ہوں

6. I am a Chemist. *maĩ chemist hũ* मैं chemist हूँ। میں کیمسٹ ہوں

7. It is good. *yah achhā hai* यह अच्छा है। یہ اچھا ہے

8. I am an Inspector. *maĩ inspector hũ.* मैं inspector हूँ। میں انسپکٹر ہوں

9. She is a Midwife. *vah midwife hai.* वह midwife है। وہ مڈوائف ہے

10. He is a Conductor. *vah conductor hai.* वह conductor है। وہ کنڈکٹر ہے

11. I am alright (ok). *maĩ ṭhīk hũ.* मैं ठीक हूँ। میں ٹھیک ہوں

12. Rāma is a Tennis player. *Rām tennīs khilāḍī hai.* राम टेनिस खिलाड़ी है।

رام ٹنس کھلاڑی ہے

13. My name is Ratnākar. *merā nām Ratnākar hai.* मेरा नाम रत्नाकर है।

میرا نام رتنا کر ہے

7.2 USING URDU PLURAL WORDS

RATNAKAR'S FIRST THREE NOBLE TRUTHS : (Singular to Plural)

FIRST TRUTH : If the word is Masculine ending in ā (आ), the ā (आ) changes to e (ए) in plural.

eg∘ singular m∘ Boy लड़का *laḍkā* لڑکا → plural m∘ Boys लड़के *laḍke* لڑکے

SECOND TRUTH : If the word is Feminine ending in a consonant, then ẽ (एँ) is added in plural.

eg∘ singular f∘ Book किताब *kitāb* کتاب → plural f∘ Books किताबें *kitābẽ* کتابیں

THIRD TRUTH : If the word is Feminine ending in ī (ई), the ī (ई) changes to iyã (इयाँ) in plural.

e.g. Singular f∘ Girl लड़की *laḍkī* → plural f∘ Girls लड़कियाँ *laḍkiyã* لڑکیاں

MORE EXAMPLES : (* = no change)

Singular					PLURAL			
Dog (m∘)	कुत्ता	*(kuttā)*	کتا	→	Dogs	कुत्ते	*(kutte)*	کتے
Cat (f∘)	बिल्ली	(billī)	بلی	→	Cats	बिल्लियाँ	*(billiyā̃)*	بلیاں
Car (f∘)	गाड़ी	*(gāḍī)*	گاڑی	→	Cars	गाड़ियाँ	*(gāḍiyā̃)*	گاڑیاں
*House (m∘)	घर	*(ghar)*	گھر	→	Houses	घर	*(ghar)*	گھر
Thing (f∘)	चीज	*(chīj)*	چیز	→	Things	चीजें	*(chīje̐)*	چیزیں
Cow(f∘)	गाय	*(gāy)*	گائے	→	Cows	गाएँ	*(gāe̐)*	گائیں
*Teacher (m∘)	उस्ताद	*(ustād)*	استاد	→	Teachers	उस्ताद	*(ustād)*	استاد

PLURALS

We are boys	हम लड़के हैं	*ham laḍke haĩ*	ہم لڑکے ہیں
You are boys	आप लड़के हैं	*āp laḍke haĩ*	آپ لڑکے ہیں
They are boys	वह लड़के हैं	*vah laḍke haĩ*	وہ لڑکے ہیں
These are boys	यह लड़के हैं	*ye laḍke haĩ*	یہ لڑکے ہیں
We are girls	हम लड़कियाँ हैं	*ham laḍkiyā̃ haĩ*	ہم لڑکیاں ہیں
You are girls	आप लड़कियाँ हैं	*āp laḍkiyā̃ haĩ*	آپ لڑکیاں ہیں
They are girls	वह लड़कियाँ हैं	*vah laḍkiyā̃ haĩ*	وہ لڑکیاں ہیں
These are girls	यह लड़कियाँ हैं	*ye laḍkiyā̃ haĩ*	یہ لڑکیاں ہیں

EXERCISE *mashq* (مشق मश्क) 41 :

Translate the English sentences into Urdu (Answers are given for help)

1. We are men. *ham ādamī hai̐.* हम आदमी हैं। ہم آدمی ہیں

2. We are women. *ham aurate̐ hai̐.* हम औरतें हैं। ہم عورتیں ہیں

3. This is a house. *yah ghar hai.* यह घर है। یہ گھر ہے

4. Those are houses. *vah ghar hai̐.* वह घर हैं। وہ گھر ہیں

5. This is a dog. *yah kuttā hai.* यह कुत्ता है। یہ کتا ہے

6. Those are dogs. *vah kutte hai̐.* वह कुत्ते हैं। وہ کتے ہیں

7. That is a cat. *vah billī hai.* वह बिल्ली है। وہ بلی ہے

8. These are cats. *yah billiyā̃ hai̐.* यह बिल्लियाँ हैं। یہ بلیاں ہیں

9. You are a Painter. (*āp painter hai̐.* आप पेन्टर हैं) آپ پینٹر ہیں

10. These are Urdu books. (*yah Urdu kitābe̐ hai̐.* ये उर्दू किताबें हैं) یہ اردو کتابیں ہیں

11. Those are red cars. (*vah lāl gādiyā̃ hai̐.* वह लाल गाड़ियाँ हैं) وہ لال گاڑیاں ہیں

12. Those cars are red. (*vah gādiyā̃ lāl hai̐.* वह गाड़ियाँ लाल हैं) وہ گاڑیاں لال ہیں

13. Khān is a Weaver. (*Khān julāhā hai.* खान जुलाहा है) خاں جولاہا ہے

14. She is an Indian. (*vah Hindustanī hai.* वह हिंदुस्तानी है) وہ ہندوستانی ہے

15. You are American. (*āp Amrican hai̐.* आप अमरीकन हैं) وہ امریکن ہے

16. They are Chinese. (*vah Chīnī hai̐.* वह चीनी हैं) وہ چینی ہیں

7.3 SPEAKING A <u>PAST EVENT</u> - 'WAS' (था) تھا

Key words: Here = ***yahā̃*** यहाँ یہاں , There = ***vahā̃*** वहाँ وہاں , Where = ***kahā̃*** कहाँ کہاں

Rich =***amīr*** अमीर امیر, Poor= ***gharīb*** ग़रीब غریب , Don't =मत مت, Up to = ***tak*** तक تک

نقشہ TABLE 2 : Speaking Past Events

Subject		was (m∘)	was (f∘)	were (m∘)	were (f∘)
I	मैं *maĩ* میں	था *thā* تھا	थी *thī* تھی		
He	वह *vah* وہ	था *thā* تھا			
She	वह *vah* وہ		थी *thī* تھی		
We	हम *ham* ہم			थे *the* تھے	थीं *thĩ* تھیں
You	आप *āp* آپ			थे *the* تھے	थीं *thĩ* تھیں
You	तुम *tum* تم			थे *the* تھے	थीं *thĩ* تھیں
You	तू *tū* تو		थी *thī* تھی	था *thā* تھا	थी *thī* تھی
They	वह *vah* وہ			थे *the* تھے	थीं *thĩ* تھیں
These	यह *yah* یہ			थे *the* تھے	थीं *thĩ* تھیں

NOTE : The above table shoes that :

(i) Suffixes for the Past events are *thā, thī, the, thĩ* (था थी थे थीं)

تھا , تھی , تھے , تھیں

(ii) Ending *'ā'* (आ) stands for masculine gender, singular subject (I, you, he) See examples below

(iv) Ending *'ī'* (ई) shows a feminine singular subject (I, she) See examples below

(v) Ending *'e'* (ए) stands for masculine plural subject (we, you, they) See examples below

(vi) Ending letter *'ĩ'* (ईं) stands for feminine plural subject (we, you, they) See examples below

* In Urdu and Hindi there is no Neuter gender, all English Neuter things are Masculine or Feminine.

Masculine

I was	मैं था	*maĩ thā*	میں تھا
We were	हम थे	*ham the*	ہم تھے
You were	आप थे	*āp the*	آپ تھے
Where were you	आप कहाँ थे?	*āp kahā̃ the?*	آپ کہاں تھے؟
He was here	वह यहाँ था	*vah yahā̃ thā*	وہ یہاں تھا
They were here	वह यहाँ थे	*vah yahā̃ the*	وہ یہاں تھے
* It was here	यह यहाँ था	*yah yahā̃ thā*	یہ یہاں تھا
These were here	यह यहाँ थे	*yah yahā̃ the*	یہ یہاں تھے
I was poor	मैं ग़रीब था	*maĩ garīb thā*	میں غریب تھا
He was rich	वह अमीर था	*vah amīr thā*	وہ امیر تھا

Feminine

I was	मैं थी	*maĩ thī*	میں تھی
We were	हम थीं	*ham thĩ*	ہم تھیں
You were	आप थीं	*āp thĩ*	آپ تھیں
Where were you	आप कहाँ थीं?	*āp kahā̃ thĩ?*	آپ کہاں تھیں؟
She was here	वह यहाँ थी	*vah yahā̃ thī*	وہ یہاں تھی
They were here	वह यहाँ थीं	*vah yahā̃ thĩ*	وہ یہاں تھیں
* It was here	यह यहाँ थी	*yah yahā̃ thī*	یہ یہاں تھی
These were here	यह यहाँ थीं	*yah yahā̃ thĩ*	یہ یہاں تھیں

I was poor	मैं ग़रीब थी	*maĩ garīb thī*	میں غریب تھی
She was rich	वह अमीर थी	*vah amīr thī*	وہ امیر تھی

NOTE : In urdu, the Question Mark is ؟ placed at the end of the Urdu sentence.

EXERCISE *mashq* (مشق मश्क) 42 : Present tense and Past tense

Translate the English sentences into Urdu (Answers are given for help)

Key Words : Not = ***nahĩ*** **नहीं** **نہیں**, And = ***aur*** **और** **اور** , Or = ***yā*** **या** **یا** ,

Also = ***bhī*** **भी** **بھی**, Only = ***hī*** **ही** **ہی**

1. I was an engineer. ***main engineer thā.*** **मैं engineer था।** **میں انجینئر تھا**
2. He was dentist. ***vah dātõ ka dākṭr thā.*** **द्वाह दातों का डाक्टर था।** **وہ داتوں کا ڈاکٹر تھی**
3. Where was she? ***vah kahā̃ thī.*** **वह कहाँ थी।** **وہ کہاں تھی؟**
4. He is a thief. ***vah chor hai.*** **वह चोर है।** **وہ چور ہے**
5. They are thieves. ***vah chor haĩ.*** **वह चोर हैं।** **وہ چور ہیں**
6. You were there. ***āp vahā̃ the.*** **आप वहाँ थे।** **آپ وہاں تھے**

7.4 USING THE ACTION WORDS FOR MAKING YOUR OWN SENTENCES

Let us learn how to make our own sentences **in the following five ways**

1. I normally 'do' (habitual) (you do; he, she, it does; we do, they do) see - Table 3
2. I am 'doing' (you are doing; he, she, it is doing; we, they are doing) Table 4
3. I was 'doing' (you were doing; he, she, it was doing; they were doing) Table 5
5. I had 'already' done (you had done; he, she, it had done; we, they had done) Table 6

6. I 'used to do' (you used to do; he, she, it used to do; they used to do) Table 7

نقشہ TABLE 3 : Making sentences with - I do; you do; he, she, we do; they do.

Doer of the action — drink — am, is, are, has, have

Subject		Verb Masculine	Verb Feminine	Present tense
I drink	मैं *maĩ* میں	पीता *pītā* پیتا	पीती *pītī* پیتی	हूँ *hũ* ہوں
He drinks	वह *vah* وہ	पीता *pītā* پیتا		है *(hai)* ہے
She drinks	वह *vah* وہ		पीती *pītī* پیتی	है *(hai)* ہے
We drink	हम *ham* ہم	पीते *pīte* پیتے	पीती *pītī* پیتی	हैं *(haĩ)* ہیں
You drink	आप *āp* آپ	पीते *pīte* پیتے	पीती *pītī* پیتی	हैं *(haĩ)* ہیں
You drink	तुम *tum* تم	पीते *pīte* پیتے	पीती *pītī* پیتی	हो *(ho)* ہو
You drink	तू *tū* تو	पीता *pītā* پیتا	पीती *pītī* پیتی	है *(hai)* ہے
They drink	वह *vah* وہ	पीते *pīte* پیتے	पीती *pītī* پیتی	हैं *(haĩ)* ہیں

EXERCISE *mashq* (مشق मश्क) 43 : Present Habitual mode

Translate the English sentences into Urdu (Answers are given for help)

1. I drink tea. *maĩ chāy pītā (pītī) hũ* मैं चाय पीता (पीती) हूँ।

میں چائے پیتی ہوں   میں چائے پیتا ہوں

You drink tea. *āp chāy pīte haĩ.* आप चाय पीते हैं। آپ چائے پیتے ہیں

He drinks tea. *vah chāy pītā hai.* वह चाय पीता है। وہ چائے پیتا ہے

2. She eats hot Samosās *vah garam samose khatī hai* वह गरम समोसे खाती है।

وہ گرم سموسے کھاتی ہے

We walk 10 km. *hum das km chalte haĩ.* हम 10 *km.* चलते हैं। ہم دس کلومیٹر چلتے ہیں

They drink hot tea. *vah garam chāy pīte haĩ.* वह गरम चाय पीते हैं। وہ گرم چائے پیتے ہیں

3. They eat bananas. *vah kele khāte haĩ.* वह केले खाते हैं। وہ کیلے کھاتے ہیں

4. She sleeps at 10 O Clock. *vah das baje sotī hai* वह दस बजे सोती है। وہ دس بجے سوتی ہے

5. You write books. *āp kitābẽ likhte haĩ.* आप किताब लिखते हैं। آپ کتابیں لکھتے ہیں

6. He goes home. *vah ghar jātā hai.* वह घर जाता है। وہ گھر جاتا ہے

نقشہ TABLE 4 : Use of, I am doing; you are doing; he, she is doing; we are doing; they are doing

Doer of the action — Doing (verb drink = पी *pī*) — I am, he is, they are

I am drinking etc.		Verb Masculine : xxxing	Verb Feminine : xxxing	
I	मैं *maĩ* میں	पी रहा *pī rahā* پی رہا	पी रही *pī rahī* پی رہی	हूँ *hũ* ہوں
He	वह *vah* وہ	पी रहा *pī rahā* پی رہا		है *(hai)* ہے
She	वह *vah* وہ		पी रही *pī rahī* پی رہی	है *(hai)* ہے
We	हम *hum* ہم	पी रहे *pī rahe* پی رہے	पी रही *pī rahī* پی رہی	हैं *(haĩ)* ہیں
You	आप *āp* آپ	पी रहे *pī rahe* پی رہے	पी रही *pī rahī* پی رہی	हैं *(haĩ)* ہیں
You	तुम *tum* تم	पी रहे *pī rahe* پی رہے	पी रही *pī rahī* پی رہی	हो *(ho)* ہو
You	तू *tū* تو	पी रहा *pī rahā* پی رہا	पी रही *pī rahī* پی رہی	है *(hai)* ہے
They	वह *vah* وہ	पी रहे *pī rahe* پی رہے	पी रही *pī rahī* پی رہی	हैं *(haĩ)* ہیں

*NOTE : Masculine Plural verb can be is used for Feminine Plural verb also.

e.g. पी रहे *pī rahe* پی رہے for पी रही *pī rahī* پی رہی

EXERCISE *mashq* (مشق मश्क) 44 : Present Continuous mode

Translate the English sentences into Hindī (Answers are given for help)

1. I am drinking tea *mai chāy̆ pī rahā (rahī) hũ.* मैं चाय पी रहा (रही) हूँ।

میں چائے پی رہا ہوں، میں چائے پی رہی ہوں

2. They are eating bananas. *vah kele khā rahe haĩ.* वह केले खा रहे हैं। وہ کیلے کھا رہے ہیں

3. She is sleeping. *vah so rahī hai.* वह सो रही है। وہ سو رہی ہے

4. You are writing. *āp likh rahe haĩ.* आप लिख रहे हैं। آپ لکھ رہے ہیں

5. He is going home. *vah ghar jā rahā hai.* वह घर जा रहा है। وہ گھر جا رہا ہے

نقشہ TABLE 5 : I was doing; you were doing; he-she was doing; we were doing; they were doing

Doer of the action — Doing (verb drink = पी *pī*)

Subj०	Verb Masculine : was drinking	Verb Feminine : was drinking
I मैं *maĩ* میں	पी रहा था *pī rahā thā* پی رہا تھا	पी रही थी *pī rahī thī* پی رہی تھی
He वह *vah* وہ	पी रहा था *pī rahā thā* پی رہا تھا	
She वह *vah* وہ		पी रही थी *pī rahī thī* پی رہی تھی
We हम *hum* ہم	पी रहे थे *pī rahe the* پی رہے تھے	पी रही थी *pī rahī thī* پی رہی تھی
You आप *āp* آپ	पी रहे थे *pī rahe the* پی رہے تھے	पी रही थी *pī rahī thī* پی رہی تھی
You तुम *tum* تم	पी रहे थे *pī rahe the* پی رہے تھے	पी रही थी *pī rahī thī* پی رہی تھی
You तू *tū* تو	पी रहा था *pī rahā thā* پی رہا تھا	पी रही थी *pī rahī thī* پی رہی تھی
They वह *vah* وہ	पी रहे थे *pī rahe the* پی رہے تھے	पी रही थी *pī rahī thī* پی رہی تھی

*NOTE : Masculine Plural verb may be used as Feminine Plural verb also. e.g. पी रहे थे *pī rahe the* پی رہے تھے for पी रही थी *pī rahī thī* پی رہی تھی

EXERCISE *mashq* (مشق मश्क) 45 : Past Continuous mode

Translate the English sentences into Hindī (Answers are given for help)

1. I was drinking tea. *maĩ chāy pī rahā thā (rahī thī).* मैं चाय पी रहा था (रही थी)।

میں چائے پی رہی تھی میں چائے پی رہا تھا

2. She was drinking tea. *vah chāy pī rahī thī.* वह चाय पी रही थी। وہ چائے پی رہی تھی

3. They were eating bananas. *vah kele khā rahe the.* वह केले खा रहे थे। وہ کیلے کھا رہے تھے

4. She was sleeping at two O Clock. *vah do baje so rahī thī.* वह दो बजे सो रही थी।

وہ دو بجے سو رہی تھی

5. He was going home. *vah ghar jā rahā thā.* वह घर जा रहा था। وہ گھر جا رہا تھا

نقشہ नक्शा TABLE 6 :

I had 'already' done, you have done; he, she has done; we, they have done

Doer of the action — Doing (verb drink = पी *pī*)

Subj°	Verb Masculine : had already drunk	Verb Feminine : had already drunk
I मैं *maĩ* میں	पी चुका था *pī chukā thā* پی چکا تھا	पी चुकी थी *pī chukī thī* پی چکی تھی
He वह *vah* وہ	पी चुका था *pī chukā thā* پی چکا تھا	
She वह *vah* وہ		पी चुकी थी *pī chukī thī* سو چکی تھی
We हम *hum* ہم	पी चुके थे *pī chuke the* پی چکے تھے	पी चुके थे *pī chuke the* آ چکے تھے
You आप *āp* آپ	पी चुके थे *jā chuke the* پی چکے تھے	पी चुके थे *pī chuke the* جا چکے تھے
You तुम *tum* تم	पी चुके थे *pī chuke the* پی چکے تھے	पी चुके थे *pī chuke the* جا چکے تھے
You तू *tū* تو	पी चुका था *pī chukā thā* پی چکا تھا	पी चुकी थी *pī chukī thī* جا چکی تھی
They वह *vah* وہ	पी चुके थे *pī chuke the* پی چکے تھے	पी चुके थे *pī chuke the* پی چکے تھے

*NOTE : Generally, Masculine Plural verb is used as Feminine Plural verb also.

EXERCISE *mashq* (مشق मश्क) 46 : Past Already Completed mode

Translate the English sentences into Hindī (Answers are given for help)

1. I had already eaten two hot Samosās. *maĩ do garam samose khā chukā thā. (chukī thī).* मैं दो गरम समोसे खा चुका था (चुकी थी)। میں دو گرم سموسے کھا چکا تھا

2. You had already read three books. *āp tīn kitābẽ paḍh chuke the.* आप तीन किताबें पढ़ चुके थे। آپ تین کتابیں پڑھ چکے تھے آپ تین کتابیں پڑھ چکی تھی

3. He had already seen Delhi. *vah Dillī dekh chukā thā.*

वह दिल्ली देख चुका था। وہ دہلی دیکھ چکا تھا

4. She had already given you the money. *vah āp ko paise de chukī thī.*

वह आप को पैसे दे चुकी थी। وہ آپ کو پیسے دے چکی تھی

5. We had already caught the cat. *hum billiyon ko pakaḍ chuke the.*

हम बिल्ली पकड़ चुके थे। ہم بلا پکڑ چکے تھے

6. They had already sung the songs. *vah gāne gā chuke the.* वह गाने गा चुके थे।

وہ گانے گا چکی تھی   وہ گانے گا چکے تھے

نقشہ नक्शा TABLE 7 :

I used to do; you used to do; he/she used to do; we used to do; they used to do

Doer of the action — Doing (verb drink = पी *pī*)

Subj.	Verb Masculine : Used to drink	Verb Feminine : Used to drink
I मैं *maĩ* میں	पीता था *pītā thā* پیتا تھا	पीती थी *pī rahī thī* پیتی تھی
He वह *vah* وہ	पीता था *pītā thā* پیتا تھا	
She वह *vah* وہ		पीती थी *pī rahī thī* پیتی تھی
We हम *hum* ہم	आते थे *āte the* آتے تھے	आती थी *ātī thī* آتی تھی *
You आप *āp* آپ	जाते थे *jāte the* جاتے تھے	जाती थी *jātī thī* جاتی تھی
You तुम *tum* تم	जाते थे *jāte the* جاتے تھے	जाती थी *jātī thī* جاتی تھی
You तू *tū* تو	जाता था *jātā thā* جاتا تھا	जाती थी *jātī thī* جاتی تھی
They वह *vah* وہ	पीते थे *pīte the* پیتے تھے	पीती थी *pī rahī thī* پیتی تھی

* NOTE : Masculine Plural verb may be used as Feminine Plural verb also.

EXERCISE *mashq* (مشق मश्क) 47 : Past 'used to do' mode

Translate the English sentences into Hindī (Answers are given for help)

1. I used to drink tea. *maĩ chāy pītā thā (maĩ chāy pītī thī).* मैं चाय पीता था, मैं चाय पीती थी। میں چائے پیتا تھا میں چائے پیتی تھی

2. He (she) used to drink tea. *vah chāy pītā thā.* वह चाय पीता था। *vah chāy pītī thī.*

वह चाय चाय पीता था, वह चाय पीती थी। وہ چاے پیتا تھا، وہ چاے پیتی تھی

3. They used to eat meat. *vah gosht khāte the.* वह गोश्त खाते थे। وہ گوس کھاتے تھے

4. You used to write books. *āp kitābẽ likhte the.* आप किताबें लिखते थे। آپ کتابیں لکھتے تھے

EXERCISE *mashq* (مشق मश्क) 48 : ON WHAT WE LEARNED SO FAR

Translate the Hindī sentences into English (Answers are given for help)

Key Words : O Clock, at O Clock = ***baje*** बजे بجے ; Today = ***āj*** आज آج ;

Tomorrow, Yesterday = ***kal*** कल کل ; Now = ***ab*** अब اب ; Then (at that time) =

tab तब تب ; When? = ***kab*** कब کب; What? = ***kyā*** क्या کیا; Work = ***kām*** काम کام

1. Anjalī is coming at two O Clock. *añjalī do baje ā rahī hai.*

अंजली दो बजे आ रही है। انجلی دو بجے آ رہی ہے

2. They are not working today. *vah āj kām nahī̃ kar rahe haĩ.*

वह आज काम नहीं कर रहे हैं। وہ آج کام نہیں کر رہے ہیں

3. Yesterday she was eating two *Roties.* *Vah kal do roṭiyā̃ khā rahī thī.*

वह कल दो रोटियाँ खा रही थी। کل وہ دو روساں کھا رہی تھی

4. What Ahmad Ali was saying yesterday? *Ahmad Ali kal kyā kah rahā thā.*

अहमद अली कल क्या कह रहा था? احمد علی کل کیا کہہ رہا تھا؟

5. Mīrā was singing Urdu songs. (song = *gānā*) *mīrā Urdu gāne gā rahī thī.*

मीरा उर्दू गाने गा रही थी। میرا اردو گانے گا رہی تھی

6. Rādhā wants a cup of tea. *Rādhā ek kap chāy chāhatī hai.*

राधा एक कप चाय चाहती है। رادھا ایک کپ چائے چاہتی ہے

7. Rītā is now going home. *Rītā ab ghar jā rahī hai.*

रीता अब घर जा रही है। ریتا اب گھر جا رہی ہے

8. Nītā can run 10 km. *Nītā das kilo-mitar daud̤ saktī hai.*

नीता दस किलो-मिटर दौड़ सकती है। نیتا دس کلومیٹر دوڑ سکتی ہے

9. You can not walk even one km. *āp ek km. bhī nahı̐ chal sakte haı̐.*

आप एक कि.मी. भी नहीं चल सकते। آپ ایک کلومیٹر بھی نہیں چل سکتے

10. Yesterday a house was burning. *kal ek ghar jal rahā thā.*

कल एक घर जल रहा था। کل ایک گھر جل رہا تھا

11. Gopāl has already fried the Samosās. *Gopāl samose tal chukā hai.*

गोपाल समोसे तल चुका है। گوپال سموسے تل چکا ہے

12. Monā had already brought the books. *Monā kitābẽ lā chukī thī.*

मोना किताबें ला चुकी थी। مونا کتابیں لا چکی تھی

13. Masood Nabi reads at 7 O Clock. *Masūd nabī sāt baje paḍhtā hai.*

मसूद नबी सात बजे पढ़ता है। مسود نبی سات بجے پڑھتا ہے

14. I used to drink only coffee, now I drink tea also. *maı̐ kāfī hī pītā thā, ab maı̐ chāy bhī pītā hū̐.* मैं काफी ही पीता था, अब मैं चाय भी पीता हूँ।

میں کافی ہی پیتا تھا اب میں چائے بھی پیتا ہوں

15. They had already played Chess. *vah shatranj khel chuke the.*

वह शतरंज खेल चुके थे। وے شطرنج کھیل چکے تھے

7.5 MAKING YOUR OWN SENTENCES FOR FUTURE EVENTS

نقشہ नक्शा TABLE 8 : Future actions : I will do, I will eat, I will go, ...etc.

Doer of the action   drink   am, is, are, has, have

Subject		Verb Masculine : will	Verb Feminine : will
I will drink	मैं *maĩ* میں	पीऊँगा *pīūngā* پیونگا	पीऊँगी *pīūngī* پیونگی
He will drink	वह *vah* وہ	पीएगा *piegā* پئےگا	
She will drink	वह *vah* وہ		पीएगी *piegī* پئےگی
We will drink	हम *hum* ہم	पीएँगे *pīenge* پئیں گے	पीएँगे *pīenge* پئیں گے *
You will drink	आप *āp* آپ	पीएँगे *pīenge* پئیں گے	पीएँगे *pīenge* پئیں گے *
You will drink	तुम *tum* تم	पीओगे *pīoge* پیوگے	पीओगी *pīogī* پیوگی
You will drink	तू *tū* تو	एगा *piegā* پئےگا	पीएगी *piegī* پئےگی
They will drink	वह *vah* وہ	पीएँगे *pīenge* پئیں گے	पीएँगे *pīenge* پئیں گے *

*NOTE : Masculine plural **forms are good enough for** Feminine plural **tenses also.**

EXERCISE *mashq* (مشق मश्क) 49 : Future Events

Translate the English sentences into Hindī (Answers are given for help)

1. I will eat a mango. *maĩ ek ām khāūngā (khāūngī).*

मै एक आम खाऊँगा (खाऊँगी)। میں ایک عام کھاوگا-میں ایک عام کھاوگی

2. You will bring the money. *āp paise lāenge.* आप पैसे लाएँगे। آپ پیسے لائیں گے

3. He (she) will wash clothes tomorrow. *vah kal kapḍe dhoegā (dhoegī).*

वह कल कपड़े धोएगा (धोएगी)। وہ کل کپڑے دھوئے گا-وہ کل کپڑے دھوئے گی

4. We will write two. *hum do khat likhenge.* हम दो खत लिखेंगे। ہم دو خط لکھیں گے

5. Will they drink wine? *vah sharāb pienge kyā?* वह शराब पीएँगे क्या? *kyā vah sharāb pienge?* क्या वह शराब पीएँगे? کیا وہ شراب پئیں گے؟ وہ شراب پئیں گے کیا؟

6. What will they ask? *vah kyā pūchhenge?* वह क्या पूछेंगे? وہ کیا پوچھیں گے؟

RATNAKAR'S FOURTH NOBLE TRUTH : ***(kyā)***

Whem '*kyā*' (क्या) comes at the beginning or at the end of a sentence, *kyā* (क्या) = a question mark (?). But, when *kyā* (क्या) comes anywhere in the sentence, then this *kyā* (क्या) = what? **See examples 5 and 6 above.**

EXERCISE *mashq* (مشق मश्क) **50 :**

Translate the Hindī sentences into English (Answers are given for help)

Key Words : Everyday = ***roz*** रोज़ روز ; Never = ***kabhī nahī̃*** कभी नहीं کبھی نہیں ;

Always = ***hameshā*** हमेशा ہمیشہ ; Someone = ***koī*** कोई کوئی ;

Ever = ***kabhī*** कभी کبھی ; Anytime = ***kabhī bhī*** कभी भी کبھی بھی ,

Some, Something = ***kuchh*** कुछ کچھ ; Anything = ***kuchh bhī*** कुछ भी کچھ بھی ;

Where = ***kahā̃*** कहाँ کہاں ; Somewhere = ***kahī̃*** कहीं کہیں ;

Anywhere = ***kahī̃ bhī*** कहीं भी کہیں بھی

1. **Neil will come home at two O Clock.** ***Neil do baje ghar āegā.***

नील दो बजे घर आएगा। نیل دو بجے گھر آئیگا

2. **Rānī will not work today.** ***Rānī āj kām nahī̃ karegī.***

रानी आज काम नहीं करेगी। رانی آج کام نہیں کریگی

3. **Yesterday Nīrā was sewing a scarf.** ***kal Nīrā dupṭṭā sī rahī thī.***

कल नीरा दुपट्टा सी रही थी। کل نیرا ڈوپٹا سی رہی تھی

4. What should Vijay say to Amir? *Vijay kyā kahe?*

विजय क्या कहे? وجے امیر سے کیا کہے؟

5. What will Mīnā say tommorrow to Razia? *Mīnā raziyā ko kal kyā kahegī?* मीना

रज़िया को कल क्या कहेगी? مینا رضیہ کو کل کیا کہے گی ؟

6. Rājā will go to the farmer's field sometime. *Rājā kisān ke khet mẽ kabhī jāyegā.*

राजा किसान के खेत में कभी जाएगा। راجہ کساں کے کھیت میں کبھی جاے گا

7. Will (should) Rīkkī go home now? *Rīkkī ab ghar jāegā kyā?*

रीक्की अब घर जाएगा क्या? رکی اب گھر جائیگا کیا؟

8. Where will Nīrū keep the Urdu books? *Nīrū Urdū kitānẽ khā̃ rakhegi?*

नीरू उर्दू किताबें कहाँ रखेगी? نیر واردو کتابیں کہاں رکھے گی؟

9. What will David write in the examination today? *David aj imtehān mẽ kyā likhegā?*

डेविड आज इम्तेहान में क्या लिखेगा? داود آج امتحاں میں کیا لکھے گا

10. What was burning yesterday? *kal kyā jal rahā thā.*

कल क्या जल रहा था। کل کیا جل رہا تھا؟

11. Raju had already washed the pots. *rājū batran dho chukā thā.*

गोविंद बरतन धो चुका था। راجو برتن دھو چکا تھا

12. Mohan will not sleep here today. *Mohan āj yahā̃ nahī̃ soyegā.*

मोहन आज यहाँ नहीं सोएगा। موہن آج یہاں نہیں سوے گا

17. Somebody was here. *koī yahā̃ thā.* यहाँ कोई था। یہاں کوئی تھا

18. Was anyone here? *koī yahā̃ thā kyā ?* कोई यहाँ था क्या? کوئی یہاں تھا کیا؟

LESSON 8

MAKING YOUR OWN SENTENCES

FOR COMPLETED ACTIONS

A perfected or completed action indicates what you did, have done or had done.

(i) suffix (m◦) *ā* (आ) or (f◦) *ī* (ई) is attached to the verb that ends in a consonant or a short vowel. eg◦ verb *chal* चल (to walk) → walked *chal + ā = chalā;* I walked m◦ *maĩ chalā,* f◦ *maĩ chalī.* चल + आ = चला, (m◦) मैं चला, (f◦) मैं चली। چل+آ=چلا؛ میں چلا، میں چلی

(ii) suffix *yā (y + ā)* या or *yī (y + ī)* यी is attached to the verb that ends in a long vowel such as *ā, ī* or *o* (आ, ई, ओ). eg◦ verb (Sleep) : *so* सो → (slept) : m◦ *so + y + ā = soyā,* I slept : m◦ *maĩ soyā,* सो + या = सोया, (m◦) मैं सोया میں سوا , f◦ *maĩ soyī.* मैं सोयी। میں سوی

(iii) If a completed action is Transitive, suffix *ne* (ने) is attached to the subject. verb (Eat) *khā* खा → (ate) *khā + yā = khāyā,* (I ate) *maĩne khāyā.* खा + या = खाया, मैंने खाया। میں نے کھایا ,

(Drink) *pī* पी → (drank) *pī + yā =* पीया *pīyā* پیا , (I drank *maĩne pīyā* मैंने पीया میں نے پیا

(iv) When suffix *ne* (ने) is attached to a subject, the verb changes according to the Object (the thing on which the action is done). Now the Subject has no effect on the verb. eg◦ m◦ and f◦ subject →

1. I ate a banana.	*maĩ ne kelā khāyā*	मैंने केला खाया	میں نے کیلا کھایا ;
2. I ate bananas.	*maĩ ne kele khāye*	मैंने केले खाये	میں نے کیلے کھائے ;
3. I ate a roṭī	*maĩ ne roṭī khāyī*	मैंने रोटी खायी	میں نے روٹی کھائی ;
4. I ate roṭīs	*maĩ ne roṭiyā̃ khāyī̃*	मैंने रोटियाँ खायीं	میں نے روٹیاں کھائیں

RATNAKAR'S FIFTH NOBLE TRUTH : **(Perfect tense)**

If an action is completed on a transitive verb, suffix *ne* (ने) is attached to the subject.

(a) Completed or perfected **action = I did, I have done, I had done ...etc.**

(b) Transitive action **is where the the action is performed on an object, not on the** subject. eg。I (the subject) ate (the verb) a mango (the object), I drank tea, I wrote a book ...etc.

(c) Intransitive action is where the action is performed by the doer (subject) on him/herself, i.e. the action is not transferred to any external object. eg。I (the subject) went, Bob slept, John walked, dog ran, cat died, they stayed, we came, you lived, baby cried, water leaked, house burnt, Sonia won, she swam, he sat, monkey jumped, sun rose, rain fell.

The perfect (completed) actions are mainly of three kinds, such as :

1. I did (you did; he, she, it did; we did; they did) see - Table 8
2. I have done (you have done; he, she has done; we have done; they have done)
3. I had done (you had done; he, she had done; we had done; they had done)

نقشہ TABLE 9 : I walked, he walked, she walked, they walked, ...etc.

A. INTRANSITIVE ACTIONS e.g. Walk = चल *chal* چل

Add suffix आ *ā* ا to the Intransitive verb

** verb Walk = चल *chal* → Walked चला *chalā* چلا

Subj。Doer of the action	Verb Masculine	Verb Feminine
I मैं *maĩ* میں	चला *chalā* چلا	चली *chalī* چلی
He वह *vah* وہ	चला *chalā* چلا	
She वह *vah* وہ		चली *chalī* چلی
We हम *hum* ہم	चले *chale* چلے	चले *chale* چلے *
You आप *āp* آپ	चले *chale* چلے	चले *chale* چلے *
You तुम *tum* تم	चले *chale* چلے	चली *chalī* چلی
You तू *tū* تو	चला *chalā* چلا	चली *chalī* چلی
They वह *vah* وہ	चले *chale* چلے	चले *chale* چلیں *

* NOTE : Generally, Masculine Plural verb is used as Feminine Plural verb also.

نقشہ TABLE 10 : I did; you did; he did, she did, it did; we did; they did ...etc.

B. TRANSITIVE ACTIONS e.g. Eat = **खा** *khā* کھا

Add suffix ने (*ne*) نے to the Subject and suffix आ (*ā*) آ to the Transitive Verb

verb Eat = खा *khā* → Ate, did eat खाया *khayā* کھایا

M. Singular : **समोसा *samosā*;** Plural : **समोसे *samose*;** F. Singular : **रोटी *roṭī*;** Plural **रोटियाँ** *roṭiyā̃*

Subj ◦ **Doer of the action**	**Object : Masculine**	**Object : Feminine**	**Number**
I मैंने *maĩ ne* میں نے	समोसा खाया	रोटी खायी	*Singular*
He उसने *us ne* اس نے	*samosā khāyā*	*Roṭī khāyī*	*objects*
She उसने *us ne* اس نے	سموسہ کھایا	روٹی کھائی	*1. Samosā*
We हमने *ham ne* ہم نے			*2. Roṭī*
You आपने *āp ne* آپ نے	.... समोसे खाये	.... रोटियाँ खायी	
You तुमने *tum ne* تم نے	*samose khāye*	*Roṭiyā̃ khāyī*	*Plural*
You तूने *tū ne* تو نے	سموسے کھائے	روٹیاں کھائی	*objects*
They उन्हों ने *unhõ ne* انہوں نے			*1. Samose* *2. Roṭiyā̃*

* NOTE : In this tense, Gender of the Verb matches with the Object (thing), not with Subjact (doer)

EXERCISE *mashq* (مشق मश्क) **51 :** Completed Actions (Perfect tense) :

Translate the English sentences into Hindī (Answers are given for help)

INTRANSITIVE **ACTIONS (Actions that do not need an object) :**

(a). Intransitive **actions, such as I came , I went, I fell, I walked :**

I walked *maĩ chalā (chalī)* मैं चला (चली) میں چلا، میں چلی ;

You fell *āp gire* आप गिरे آپ گرے ;

He-she came *vah āyā -āyī.* वह आया–आयी وہ آیا، وہ آئے ;

He went *vah gayā* वह गया وہ گیا ;

We slept *hum soye* हम सोये ہم سوئے ;

They stayed *vah rahe.* वह रहे وہ رہے .

(b). Intransitive (Present perfect), such as I have come, I have gone, I have fallen, I have walked :

I have walked. *maĩ chalā (chalī) hũ.* मैं चला (चली) हूँ।

میں چلا ہوں، میں چلی ہوں ;

You have fallen. *āp gire haĩ.* आप गिरे हैं آپ گرے ہیں ;

He has come. *vah āyā hai.* वह आया है। وہ آیا ہے ;

She has gone. *vah gayaī hai.* वह गयी है। وہ گئی ہے ;

We have slept. *hum soye haĩ.* हम सोये हैं। ہم سوئے ہیں ;

They have stayed. *vah rahe haĩ.* वह रहे हैं। وہ رہے ہیں .

(c). Intransitive (Past perfect), such as I had come, I had gone, I had fallen, I had walked :

I had walked. *maĩ chalā (chalī) thī* मैं चला था (चली थी)

میں چلا تھا ; میں چلی تھی

You had fallen. *āp gire the.* आप गिरे थे। آپ گرے تھے ;

He had come. *vah āyā thā.* वह आया था। وہ آیا تھا ;

She had gone. *vah gayaī thī.* वह गयी थी। وہ گئی تھی ;

We had slept. *hum soye the.* हम सोये थे। ہم سوئے تھے ;

They had stayed. *vah rahe the.* वह रहे थे। وہ رہے تھے .

TRANSITIVE ACTIONS (Actions that need an object) :

(d). Transitive actions, such as I did, I wrote, I drank, I saw :

I ate. *maĩ ne khāyā.* मैंने खाया। میں نے کھایا ;

I ate a mango. *maĩ ne ām khāyā.* मैंने आम खाया। میں نے آم کھایا ;

I ate one banana. *maĩ ne ek kelā khāyā.* मैंने एक केला खाया। میں نے ایک کیلا کھایا ;

He ate two bananas. *us ne do kele khāye.* उसने दो केले खाये। اس نے دو کیلے کھائے

You ate one Roṭī. *āp ne ek Roṭī khāyī.* आपने एक रोटी खायी।

آپ نے ایک روٹی کھائی ;

They ate two Roṭīs. *ubhõ ne do Roṭiyā̃ khāyī.* उन्होंने दो रोटियाँ खायी।

اس نے دو روٹیاں کھائیں

Sharif drank tea. *Sharif ne chāy pī.* शरीफ़ ने चाय पी। شریف نے چائے پی

Jack washed hands. *Jack ne hāth dhoye.* जैक ने हाथ धोये।

جیک نے ہاتھ دھوئے ;

Sunitā watched TV. *Sunita ne TV dekhā.* सुनीता ने टीवी देखा। سونیتا نے ٹی وی دیکھا

We peeled the bananas. *hamne kele chhīle.* हमने केले छीले। ہم نے کیلے چھیلے ;

Rām and Shyām did the work. *Rām aur Shyām ne kām kiyā.* राम और शाम ने काम किया । رام اور سام نے کام کیا

(e) Transitive actions, such as - I have done, I have written, I have drunk, I have seen :

Present Perfect : I have eaten. *maĩ ne khāyā hai.* मैंने खाया है। میں نے کھایا ہے ;

I have eaten a mango. *maĩ ne ām khāyā hai.* मैंने आम खाया है।

میں نے ایک آم کھایا ہے ;

I have eaten one banana. *maĩ ne ek kelā khāyā hai.* मैंने एक केला खाया है।

میں نے ایک کیلا کھایا ہے ;

I have eaten two bananas. *maĩ ne do kele khāye haĩ.* मैंने दो केले खाये हैं।

میں نے دو کیلے کھائے ہیں ;

I have eaten one roṭī. *maĩ ne ek roṭī khāyī hai.* मैंने एक रोटी खायी है।

میں نے ایک روٹی کھائی ہے ;

I have eaten two roṭīs. *maĩ ne do roṭiyā̃ khāyī̃ haĩ.* मैंने दो रोटियाँ खायीं हैं।

میں نے دو روٹیاں کھائیں ہیں

(f). Transitive actions, such as - I had done, I had written, I had drunk, I had seen :

Past Perfect : I had eaten. *maĩ ne khāyā thā.* मैंने खाया था। میں نے کھایا تھا ;

I had eaten a mango *maĩ ne ām khāyā tha* मैंने आम खाया था।

میں نے ع آم کھایا تھا

I had eaten one banana. *maĩ ne ek kelā khāyā thā.* मैंने एक केला खाया था।

میں نے ایک کیلا کھایا تھا ;

I had eaten two bananas. *maĩ ne do kele khāye the.* मैंने दो केले खाये थे।

میں نے دو کیلے کھائے تھے ;

I had eaten one roṭī. *maĩ ne ek roṭī khāyī thī.* मैंने एक रोटी खायी थी।

میں نے ایک روٹی کھائی تھی

I had eaten two roṭīs. *maĩ ne do roṭiyā̃ khāyī̃ thī̃.* मैंने दो रोटियाँ खायीं थीं।

میں نے دو روٹیاں کھیں تھیں

LESSON 9

RATNAKAR'S BRAIN SURGERY OF THE URDU GRAMMAR

From the charts of tenses we studied in previous lessons, following facts can be discovered :

subject | verb and its mode | tense & person | #1 verb | #2 mode

(1) I drink hot tea = *maĩ garam chāy pītā hū̃* = maĩ میں garam گرم chāy چائے pītā پیتا hū̃ ہوں

subject | verb | adjectiv | object | adjectiv | object | #3 gender and number | #4 present tense | #5 person

Note: #2 *'t'* = habitual mode (do), *rah* = incomplete mode (-ing), *chuk* = 'already done' mode.

#3 *ā* = m∘ singular; *ī* = f∘ singular, *e* = m∘ plural; *ĩ* = f∘ plural.

#5 *ū̃* = **1st person singular; *ai, e* = second and third person singular;** *aĩ, ẽ* = plural.

(2) I was drinking tea = *maĩ chāy pī rahā thā* = maĩ میں chāy چائے pī پی rahā رہا thā تھا

#2 mode | #3 gender, number | #3 gender, | #6 past tense

Note : #6 '*th*' = was, had, *used to

*** used to = #2 + #3 and #6 + #3** (*t + ā, th + ā*)

Therefore, m\ (i) Was = *thā* था تھا (ii) Had = *thā* था تھا (iii) Used to = *tā thā* ता था تا تھا

(3) I will drink tea = *maĩ chāy pīū̃gā* = maĩ میں chāy چائے pīungā پیونگا

Note : #7 for future tense, logically the Tense operative 'g' goes after #5 Person indicator.

#1 verb | #7 future tense | #3 gender and number

(4) **I should drink tea (the Potential mood) =** *maĩ chāy pīū̃* = maĩ میں chāy چائے pīū̃ پیوں

Note : Potential mood needs only #5. It does not need any tense operative such as, h for present, th for past or g for future tense.

#5 person

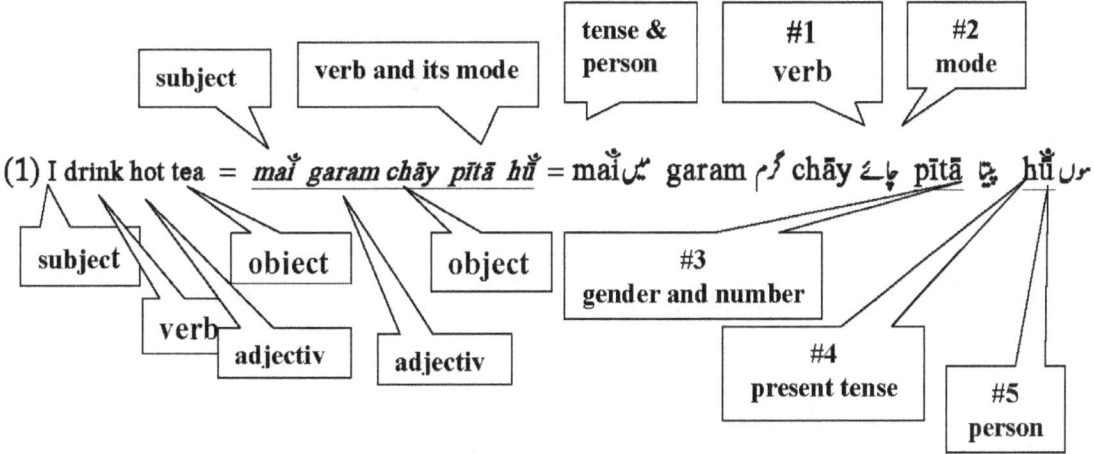

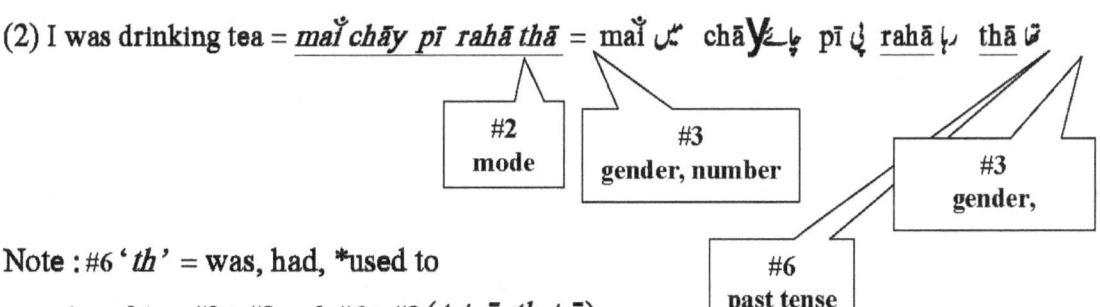

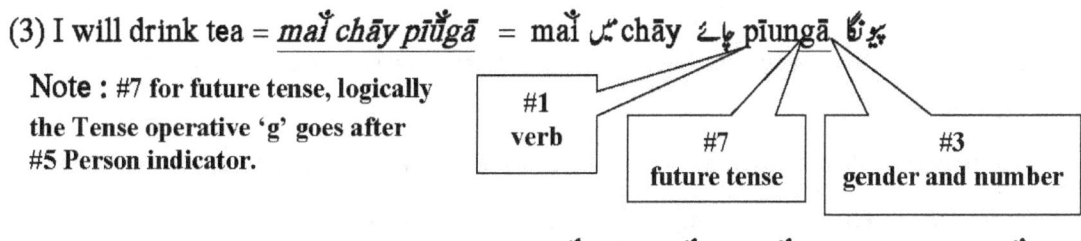

(5) I walked = I did walk = *maĩ chalā* = maĩ میں chalā چلا

perfect, intransitive verb | indefinite, perfect | subject | intransitive verb | #3 perfect tense suffix, gender and number See the Note below

Note : #3 The perfect tense suffix *ā* (आ) changes with gender (m◦ ā आ, f◦ ī ई) and number (pl◦ e ए, ī ई). Also, when the verb ends with a long vowel, (such as *ā, ī, o* आ, ई, ओ) letter *y* य is prefixed to the perfect tense suffix *ā* (आ) eg◦ (1) 'chal' *ā* = chalā چلا)2) 'so' y + ā = soyā سویا

(6) I have walked slowly = *maĩ dhīre chalā hũ* = maĩ میں dhīre دھیرے chalā چلا hũ ہوں

#5 perso | present | perfect action | subject | intransitive verb | #3 perfect tense suffix, yā for a long vowel | #4 present | adver | adver

Note : The first-person Present-perfect-tense indicator 'have' translates into Hindī as *'hũ'* हूँ

(7) I had walked = *maĩ chalā thā* = maĩ میں chalā چلا thā تھا

#3 gender and number | past | perfect action | subject | intransitive | #3 perfect tense suffix, yā for a long vowel | #6 past

Note : →6 Past tense suffix '*th*' थ is added is added to the verb ONLY when there is 'was,' 'had' or 'used to' in the sentence.

#4 present

(8) I saw (have seen, had seen) = *maĩ ne dekhā (hai, thā)* = maĩ میں ne نے dekhā دیکھا (hai, thā) تھا , ہے

perfect, transitive action | present tense | past tense | #8 transitive perfect action suffix | #3 perfect tense suffix, yā for a long vowel | #6 past

Note : →8 When the action is transitive and perfected (Simple, Present, Past or Future), suffix '*ne*' (ने) is attached to the verb.

With suffix *ne* (ने), the Subject has no effect on the verb. Now, the Object affects the verb. eg◦ (1) m◦ *Rām chāy pītā hai,* f◦ *Sītā chāy pītī hai.2)* سیتا چائے پیتی ہے). Perfect actions (Objects f. *chāy* m. *ām*) *Rām ne chāy pī, Sītā ne chāy pī, Rām ne ām khāyā, Sītā ne ām khāyā.*

رام نے چائے پی، سیتا نے چائے پی، رام نے آم کھایا، سیتا نے آم کھایا

LESSON 10

USE OF THE CASE SUFFIXES

ko (को) کو = to; *se* (से) سے = with, by, from;

mẽ (में) میں = in; *par* (पर) پر = on, at

RATNAKAR'S EIGHTH NOBLE TRUTH : **(attaching Case suffixes)**

(i) When ANY SUFFIX (*ko* को کو ; *se* से سے ; *mẽ* में میں ; *par* पर پر or any other suffix comes after a MASCULINE SINGULAR noun ending in *ā* (आ), this *ā* (आ) is changed to *e* (ए). **e.g. m∘ boy *laḍkā* लड़का + *ko* को = *laḍke ko* लड़के को।** لڑکے کو

(ii) When ANY SUFFIX comes after ANY PLURAL NOUN, particle *õ* (ओं) must be added to that noun, before attaching that suffix. **e.g.**

m∘ boys	***laḍkā + õ + ko***	=	***laḍkõ ko***	**लड़का**	**+ ओं + को**	=	**लड़कों को।**	لڑکوں کو
m∘ Houses	***ghar + õ + ko***	=	***gharõ ko***	**घर**	**+ ओं + को**	=	**घरों को।**	گھروں کو
f∘ books	***kitāb + õ + ko***	=	***kitābõ ko***	**किताब**	**+ ओं + को**	=	**किताबों को।**	کتابوں کو
f∘ Girls	***laḍkī + õ + ko***	=	***laḍkiyõ ko***	**लड़की**	**+ ओं + को**	=	**लड़कियों को।**	لڑکیوں کو

RATNAKAR'S NINTH NOBLE TRUTH **(see pronouns Table↓) :**

I = *maĩ* मैं میں ; He, she, that = *vah* वह وہ ; It, this = *yah* यह یہ

They, those = *vah* वह وہ ; These = *ye* यह یہ .

When any suffix is attached to these pronouns :

(i) *maĩ*	मैं میں	**changes to →** *muz* मुझ	مجھ
(ii) *vah*	वह وہ	**changes to →** *us* उस	اس
(iii) *yah*	यह یہ	**changes to →** *is* इस	اس
(iv) *vah* (plural)	वह وہ	**changes to →** *un* उन	ان ;
(v) *yah* (plural)	यह یہ	**changes to →** *in* इन	ان

(10.1) Use of *ko* को (to) : کو

1. I am giving a book to Ahmad. *main Ahmad ko kitāb de rahā hū̃.* میں احمد کو کتاب دے رہا ہوں

2. He is giving money to Dani. *vah Danī ko paise de rahā hai* وہ دانی کو پیسے دے رہا ہے.

3. Ali was giving keys to Mīnā. *Alī Mīnā ko chābiyā̃ de rahā thā.* علی منا کو چابیاں دے رہا تھا

4. The boys are giving bananas to the monkeys. *laḍke bandarõ ko kele de rahe hai̇̃.*

لڑکے بندروں کو کیلے دے رہے تھے

(10.2) Use of *se* से (with, by or from) : سے

(i) *se* से = WITH or BY : سے

1. I go by car. *mai̇̃ car se jātā hū̃.* मैं कार से जाता हूँ। میں کار سے جاتا ہوں

We will go by car. हम कार से जएँगे। *hum kār se jāenge.* ہم کار سے جائنگے

2. I cut bananas with a knife. *mai̇̃ chākū se kele kāṭatā hū̃.* मैं चाकू से केले काटता हूँ ।

میں چاقو سے کیلے کاٹتا ہوں

(ii) *se* से = FROM : سے

1. Muhammad came from Singāpur. *muhammad Singāpur se āyā.* محمد سنگاپور سے آیا

2. Ranī is here from four O Clock. *Rānī yahā̃ chār baje se hai* رانی یہاں چار بجے سے ہے.

(10.3) Use of *mẽ* में (in) میں and *par* पर (on, at) : پر

(i) *mẽ* में = IN میں

1. Anil is not in the room. *Anil kamre mẽ nahī̃ hai.* انیل کمرے میں نہیں ہے

3. The key is in the lock. *chābī tāle mẽ hai.* चाबी ताले में है। چابی تالے میں ہے

(ii)*par* पर = ON, AT پر

1. The cup is on the dish. *cup thālī par hai.* कप थाली पर है। کپ تھالی پر ہے

2. There are leaves on the tree. *ped par patte haĩ.* पेड़ पर पत्ते हैं। پیڑ پر پتے ہیں

(10.4) Use of *kā, kī* (का, की) کا، کی

m∘ *kā* (का) کا, f∘ *kī* (की) کی = of

The English preposition 'OF' becomes postposition *kā* (का) کا or *kī* (की) in Urdu. For showing the possessive relationship of a Masculine Object, suffix *kā* (का) کا is added to the possessor, and for a Feminine Object, suffix *kī* (की) کی is added. NOTE: This suffix is NOT controlled by the Subject, even though it is attached to the subject. This suffis is controlled by the Object.

EXAMPLES :

1. Rita's brother. *Rītā kā bhaī.* رام کا بھائی ;

Gītā's sister. *Gītā kī bahen* . گیتا کی بہن

2. This is Monika's house. *yaha Monikā kā ghar hai.* یہ مونیکا کا گھر ہے

NOTE : For first person ('my' and 'our'), suffixes *rā, rī* रा, री را، ری *are used in place of kā, kī* का, की کا، کی

EXAMPLES :

Our house. ***hamārā ghar.*** हमारा घर। ہمارا گھر

My mother. ***merī mā̃*** मेरी माँ। میری ماں

My dogs. ***mere kutte.*** मेरे कुत्ते। میرے کتے

Our dogs. ***hamāre kutte.*** हमारे कुत्ते। ہمارے کتے

Our dog. ***hamārā kuttā.*** हमारा कुत्ता। ہمارا کتا

Our cat. ***hamārī billī.*** हमारी बिल्ली। ہماری بلی

Our cats. ***hamārī billiyā̃.*** हमारी बिल्लियाँ। ہماری بلیاں

My cats. ***merī billiyā̃.*** मेरी बिल्लियाँ। میری بلیاں

(10.5) Use of suffixes ***ke sāth*** (के साथ), ***ke pās*** (के पास), ***ke liye*** (के लिये)

ke sāth (के साथ) کے ساتھ = together with; ***ke pās*** (के पास) کے پاس = near, ***ke liye*** (के लिये) کے لیے = for

(A) *ke sāth* के साथ = with, together with : کے ساتھ

(1) I am going with Sunīl. ***maĩ Sunīl ke sāth jā rahā hũ*** میں سنیل کے ساتھ جا رہا ہوں

(2) Jim will go to Karachi with Khan. *Jim khān ke sāth Karāchī jāegā* جم کل کراچی جائے گا

(B) *ke pās* के पास = with, near, have, has, had : کے پاس

(1) The money is with Dani (Dani has the money). *Paise Danī ke pās haĩ* پیسے دانی کے پاس ہیں۔

(2) Śrī Laṅkā is near India. *Śrī Lakṅkā Bhārat ke pās hai* سری لنکا بھارت کے پاس ہے

نقشہ नक्शा TABLE 11 - CHART OF SUFFIXES FOR NOUNS

NOTES : When any suffix is attached to :

(i) m∘ **SINGULAR noun ending in** आ *(ā)*, **this** आ *(ā)* is changed to ए *(e)* ے ;

(ii) any PLURAL noun (m∘ or f∘), ओं *(ō̃)* وں **is added, before attaching suffix.**

Suffeix	Singular m∘ (i) a boy, (i) लड़का لڑکا	Plural m∘ (ii) boys, (ii) लड़के لڑکے	Singular f∘ (iii) a girl (iii) लड़की لڑکی	Plural m∘ (iv) girls (iv) लड़कियाँ لڑکیاں
ने	लड़के ने ***laḍke ne*** لڑکے نے	लड़कों ने ***laḍkō̃ ne*** لڑکوں نے	लड़की ने ***laḍkī ne*** لڑکی نے	लड़कियों ने ***laḍkiyō̃ ne*** لڑکیوں نے
को	लड़के को ***laḍke ko*** لڑکے کو	लड़कों को ***laḍkō̃ ko*** لڑکوں کو	लड़की को ***laḍkī ko*** لڑکی کو	लड़कियों को ***laḍkiyō̃ ko*** لڑکیوں کو
से	लड़के से ***laḍke se*** لڑکے سے	लड़कों से ***laḍkō̃ se*** لڑکوں سے	लड़की से ***laḍkī se*** لڑکی سے	लड़कियों से ***laḍkiyō̃ se*** لڑکیوں سے
का	लड़के का ***laḍke ka*** لڑکے کا	लड़कों का ***laḍkō̃ ka*** لڑکوں کا	लड़की का ***laḍkī ka*** لڑکی کا	लड़कियों का ***laḍkiyō̃ ka*** لڑکیوں کا
में	लड़के में ***laḍke mẽ*** لڑکے میں	लड़कों में ***laḍkō̃ mẽ*** لڑکوں میں	लड़की में ***laḍkī mẽ*** لڑکی میں	लड़कियों में ***laḍkiyō̃ mẽ*** لڑکیوں میں
पर	लड़के पर ***laḍke par*** لڑکے پر	लड़कों पर ***laḍkō̃ par*** لڑکوں پر	लड़की पर ***laḍkī par*** لڑکی پر	लड़कियों पर ***laḍkiyō̃ par*** لڑکیوں پر

THE PRONOUNS

DEFINITIONS :

(1)The word used in place of a noun (in order to avoid its repetition) is called a *Pronoun.*

(2) If a pronoun qualifies a noun, then the pronoun is called a *Pronominal or Possessive Adjective.*

EXPLANATION :

(i) See this sentence :

Alī is going to Alī's school to see Alī's teacher and to return Alī's teacher Alī's teacher's books.

Alī Alī ke gurujī ko milne aur Alī ke gurujī kī kitābẽ Alī ke gurujī ko lauṭāne Alī ke skool jā rahā hai.

अली अली के गुरुजी को मिलने और अली के गुरुजी की किताबें अली के गुरुजी को लौटाने अली के स्कूल को जा रहा है।

علی علی کے گروجی کو ملنے اور علی کے گروجی کی کتابیں علی کے گروجی لوٹانے علی کے سکول کو جارہا ہے

It sounds improper and confusing.

(ii) Now see this one

(Same sentence can be re-written properly with the use of pronouns) :

Alī Alī is going to his school to see his teacher and to return him his books.

Alī *apane gurujī ko milane aur un kī kitābẽ un ko lauṭāne apane skool jā rahā hai.*

अली अपने गुरुजी को मिलने और उनकी किताबें उनको लौटाने अपने स्कूल जा रहा है।

علی اپنے گروجی کو ملنے اور ان کی کتابیں لوٹانے اپنے سکول جارہا ہے

Now, with the use of pronouns, it sounds proper.

نقشہ नक्शा TABLE 12 - CHART OF SUFFIXES FOR PRONOUNS

NOTES : **When any suffix is attached to :**

(i) m◦ **SINGULAR noun ending in** आ *(ā)*, **this** आ *(ā)* is changed to ए *(e)* ے ;

(ii) **any PLURAL noun (m◦ or f◦),** ओं *(ŏ)* وں **is added, before attaching suffix.**

Remember : When any suffix is attached to the pronouns :

(i) *maĭ* मैं میں **changes to →** *muz* मुझ مجھ

(ii) *vah* वह وہ **changes to →** *us* उस اس (iii) *yah* यह یہ **changes to →** *is* इस اس

(iv) *vah* (pl◦) वह وہ **changes to →** *un* उन ان ; (v) *yah* (pl◦) यह یہ **changes to →** *in* इन ان

	I *(maĭ)*	We *(hum)*	He-She *(vah)*	They *(vah)*	You *(āp)*	You *(tum)*	You *(tū)*
	मैं میں	हम ہم	वह وہ	वह وہ	आप آپ	तुम تم	तू تو
ने	मैंने *maĭ ne* میں نے	हमने *hum ne* ہم نے	उसने *us ne* اس نے	उन्हों ने *unhŏ ne* انہوں نے	आपने *āp ne* آپ نے	तुमने *tum ne* تم نے	तूने *tū ne* تو نے
को	मुझे *muzay* مجھے	हमें *hamĕ* ہمیں	उसे *use* اسے	उन्हें *unhĕ* انہیں	आपको *āp ko* آپ کو	तुम्हें *tumhĕ* تمہیں	तुझे *tuzay* تجھے
से	मुझसे *mujh se* مجھ سے	हमसे *hum se* ہم سے	उससे *us se* اس سے	उनसे *un se* ان سے	आपसे *āp se* آپ سے	तुमसे *tum se* تم سے	तुझसे *tujh se* تجھ سے
का	मेरा *merā* میرا	हमारा *hamārā* ہمارا	उसका *us kā* اس کا	उनका *un kā* ان کا	आपका *āp kā* آپ کا	तुम्हारा *tumhārā* تمہارا	तेरा *terā* تیرا
में	मुझमें *mujh mĕ* مجھ میں	हममें *hum mĕ* ہم میں	उसमें *us mĕ* اس میں	उनमें *un mĕ* ان میں	आपमें *āp mĕ* آپ میں	तुममें *tum mĕ* تم میں	तुझमें *tujh mĕ* تجھمیں
पर	मुझ पर *mujh par* مجھ پر	हम पर *hum par* ہم پر	उस पर *us par* اس پر	उन पर *un par* ان پر	आप पर *āp par* آپ پر	तुम पर *tum par* تم پر	तुझ पर *tujh par* تجھ پر

USE OF PRONOUNS AND POSSESSIVE ADJECTIVES

Review of what we learned so far, a 'cumulative learning'

EXERCISE *mashq* (مشق मश्क) **52 :** Use of Pronouns

Translate the English sentences into Hindī (Answers are provided for help)

1ST PERSON : I, We

1. I, We *(maĩ, hum)* मैं, हम। میں، ہم

2. I am. *(maĩ hũ)* मैं हूँ। میں ہوں

3. We are friends. *(hum dost haĩ)* हम दोस्त हैं। ہم دوست ہیں

4. Give me hundred Dollars. *(muzay ek sau dālar do)*

मुझे एक सौ डालर दो। مجھے ایک سو ڈالر دو

5. Tell us one thing. *(hamẽ ek bāt batāo)* हमें एक बात बताओ। ہمیں ایک بات بتاو

6. It will not be done by me. *(yah mujh se nahĩ hogā)*

यह मुझसे नहीं होगा। یہ مجھ سے نہیں ہوگا

7. It will be done by us. *(yah ham se hogā)* यह हमसे होगा। یہ ہم سے ہوگا

8. This is for me. *(yah mere liye hai)* यह मेरे लिये है। یہ میرے لیے ہے

9. Bring water for us. *(hamāre liye pānī lāo)* हमारे लिये पानी लाओ। ہمارے لئے پانی لو

10. He took money from me. *(us ne mujh se paisā liyā)*

उसने मुझसे पैसा लिया। اس نے مجھ سے پیسہ لیا

11. That is far from here. *(vah yahã se dūr hai)* वह यहाँ से दूर है। وہ یہاں سے دور ہے

12. He is my brother. *(vah merā bhāī hai)* वह मेरा भाई है। وہ میرا بھائی ہے

13. Our books. *(hamārī kitābẽ)* हमारी किताबें। ہماری کتابیں

14. Please belive in me. *(mujh par bharosā karo)* मुझ पर भरोसा करो। مجھ پر بھروسہ کرو

15. He lives in Delhi. *(vah Dillī mẽ rhta hai)* वह दिल्ली में रहता है। وہ دہلی میں رہتا ہے

16. My dogs. *mere kutte.* मेरे कुत्ते। میرے کتے

17. Our dogs. *hamāre kutte.* हमारे कुत्ते। ہمارے کتے

18. Our dog. *hamārā kuttā.* हमारा कुत्ता। ہمارا کتا

19. Our cat. *hamārī billī.* हमारी बिल्ली। ہماری بلی

20. Our cats. *hamārī billiyā̃.* हमारी बिल्लियाँ। ہماری بلوں

21. My cats. *merī billiyā̃.* मेरी बिल्लियाँ। میری بلوں

22. My car. *(merī gāḍī)* मेरी गाड़ी। میری گاری

23. My cars. *(merī gāḍiyā̃)* मेरी गाड़ियाँ। میری گاریاں

24. Our car. *(hamārī gāḍī)* हमारी गाड़ी। ہماری گاری

25. Our cars. *(hamārī gāḍiyā̃)* हमारी गाड़ियाँ। ہماری گاریاں

2ND PERSON : You

1. You, *āp* आप। آپ

2. You are. *(āp haĩ)* आप हैं। آپ ہیں

3. You are my friends. *(āp mere dost haĩ)* आप मेरे दोस्त हैं। آپ میرے دوست ہیں

4. I will give you hundred dollars. *(maĩ āp ko sau dālar dūṅgā-dūṅgī)* मैं आपको सौ

डालर दूँगा/दूँगी। میں آپ کو سو ڈالر دونگا، میں آپ کو سو ڈالر دوگی

5. I will tell you one thing. *(maĩ āp ko ek bāt batāũngā-batāũngī)* मैं आपको एक बात बताऊँगा/बताऊँगी। میں آپ کو ایک چیز بتاونگا؛ میں آپ کو ایک چیز

6. It will not be done by you. *(yah āp se nahĩ hogā)* यह आपसे नहीं होगा। یہ آپ سے نہیں ہوگا

7. Will it will be done by you? *(yah āp se hogā kyā?)*

यह आप लोगों से होगा क्या? یہ آپ سے ہوگا کیا؟

8. This tea is for you *(yah chāy āp ke liye hai)*

यह चाय आपके लिये है। یہ چائے آپ کے لیے ہے

9. I will bring water for you. *(maĩ āp ke liye pānī lāũngā-lāũngī)* मैं आप के लिये पानी लाऊँगा/लाऊँगी। لاوں گا میں آپ کے لیئے پانی ; لاوں گی میں آپ کے لیئے پانی

10. He took books from you. *(us ne āp se kitābẽ lī)*

उसने आपसे किताबें ली। اس نے آپ سے کتابیں لی

11. This is far from there. *(yah vahā̃ se dūr hai)* यह वहाँ से दूर है। یہ وہاں سے دور ہے

12. Is he your brother? *(vah āp kā bhāī hai kyā?)*

वह आपका भाई है क्या? وہ آپکا بھائی ہے کیا؟

13. Where are your books. *(āp kī kitābẽ kahā̃ haĩ?)*

आपकी किताबें कहाँ हैं? آپکی کتابیں کہاں ہیں؟

14. I believe in you. *(maĩ āp par bharosā kartā hũ)* میں آپ پر بھروسا کرتا ہوں

15. You live in Delhi. *(āp dillī mẽ rahate ho)* आप दिल्ली में रहते हो। آپ دلی میں رہتے ہو

16. Your dog. *(āp kā kuttā)* आपका कुत्ता। آپکا کتا

17. Your dogs. *(āp ke kutte)* आपके कुत्ते। آپکے کتے

18. Your car. *(āp kī gāḍī)* आपकी गाड़ी। آپ کی گاڑی

19. Your cars. *(āp kī gāḍiyā̃)* आपकी गड़ियाँ। آپ کی گاڑیاں

3RD PERSON : He, she, it, they, these, those

1. He, she, it, *vah, vah, yah.* वह, वह, यह। وہ، وہ، یہ

2. Those are friends. *(vah dost haĩ)* वह दोस्त हैं। وہ دوست ہیں

3. These are friends. *(ye dost haĩ)* ये दोस्त हैं। یہ دوست ہیں

4. Give him-her hundred dollars. *(us ko sau dalar do)* उसको सौ डालर दो। اس کو سو ڈالر دو

5. Tell them this thing. *(un ko yah bāt batāo)* उन कों यह बात बताओ। ان کو یہ بات بتاؤ

6. It will not be done by him-her. *(yah us se nahĩ hogā)*
यह उससे नहीं होगा। یہ اس سے نہیں ہوگا

7. It will be done by us. *(yah hum se hogā)* यह हमसे होगा। یہ ہم سے ہوگا

8. This is for her-him. *(yah us ke liye hai)* यह उसके लिये है। یہ اس کے لیے ہے

9. Bring water for them. *(un ke liye pānī lāo)* उनके लिये पानी लाओ। ان کے لیئے پانی لاؤ

10. He-she took money from him-her. *(us ne us se paisā liyā)* اس نے اس سے پیسے لئے

11. That is far from them. *(vah un se dūr hai)* वह उनसे दूर है। وہ ان سے دور ہے

12. He is his-her brother. *(vah us kā bhāī hai)* वह उसका भाई है। وہ اس کا بھائی ہے

13. Their books. *(un kī kitābẽ)* उनकी किताबें। ان کی کتابیں

14. Belive in him-her. *(us par bharosā karo)* उस पर भरोसा करो। اس پر بھروسہ کرو

15. He is in Delhi. *(vah dillī mẽ hai)* वह दिल्ली में है। وہ دلّی میں ہے

16. His-her dog. *(us kā kuttā)* उसका कुत्ता। اس کا کتا

17. His-her dogs. *(us ke kutte)* उसके कुत्ते। اس کے کتے

18. Their dog. *(un kā kuttā)* उनका कुत्ता। انکا کتا

19. Their dogs. *(un ke kutte)* उनके कुत्ते। انکے کتے

20. His-her car. *(us kī gāḍī)* उसकी गाड़ी। اسکی گاڑی

21. His-her cars. *(us kī gāḍiyā̃)* उसकी गाड़ियाँ। اسکی گاڑیاں

22. Their car. *(un kī gāḍī)* उनकी गाड़ी। ان کی گاڑیں

23. Their cars. *(un kī gāḍiyā̃)* उनकी गाड़ियाँ। انکی گاڑیاں

MORE EXPRESSIONS TO LEARN :

(1) Across = *us pār* (उस पार) اس پار

(2) After = *bād mẽ* (बाद में) بادمیں

(3) Again = *fir, punaḥ* (फिर) پھر

(4) Again and again = *bār bār* (बार बार) باربار

(5) Although = *hagarche* (अगरचे) اگرچہ

(6) If = *agar* (अगर) اگر

(7) Then = *fir, bād mẽ* (फिर, बाद में) پھر، بعد میں

(8) Before = *pahale* (पहले) پہلے

(9) Between = *bīch mẽ* (बीच में) بیچ میں

(10) Beyond = *us pār* (उस पार) اس پار

(11) There = *vahā̃* (वहाँ) وہاں

(12) Here = *yahā̃* (यहाँ) یہاں

(13) On this side = *idhar* (इधर) ادھر

(14) On that side = *udhar* (उधर) ادھر

(15) Where? = *kahā̃?* (कहाँ?) کہاں؟

(16) Where? = *kidhar?* (किधर?) کدھر؟

(17) Where = *jahā̃* (जहाँ) جہاں

(18) Where = *jidhar* (जिधर) جدھر

(19) Inside = *andar* (अंदर) اندر

(20) On, Over = *ūpar* (ऊपर) اوپر

LESSON 11

THE ADJECTIVES and ADVERBS

Definition : The word that describes, qualifies or adds something to a noun is an ADJECTIVE.

1. Good boy ***(achchhā laḍkā)*** **अच्छा लड़का** اچھا لڑکا
2. Good boys ***(achchhe laḍke)*** **अच्छे लड़के** اچھے لڑکے
3. Good girl ***(achchhī laḍkī)*** **अच्छी लड़की** اچھی لڑکی
4. Good girls ***(achchhī laḍkiyā̃)*** **अच्छी लड़कियाँ** اچھی لڑکیاں

The word that qualifies a verb or an adjective, is an ADVERB.

1. Eat slowly. ***(āhistā khāo)*** آہستہ کھاؤ
2. Walk fast. ***(tej chalo)*** **तेज चलो।** تیز چلو
3. Very good. ***(bahut achchhā)*** بہت اچھا
4. It is heavy. ***(yah bhārī hai)*** یہ بھاری ہے

11.1 THE ADJECTIVES

RULE : In HUrdū, the adjectives have same gender and number as the nouns they qualify.

EXERCISE *mashq* (مشق मश्क) 53 : Use of Adjectives

Translate the English sentences into Hindī (Answers are given for help)

1. Rānī does good work. ***(Rānī achchhā kām kartī hai)*** رانی اچھا کام کرتی ہے

2. The oranges are sweet. *(santare mīṭhe haĩ)* (Sweet = m◦ *mīṭhe*) سنترے میٹھے ہیں

3. We saw yellow rose. *(hum ne pīlā gulāb dekhā)* ہم نے پیلا گلاب دیکھا

4. Eat your own food. *(apanā khānā khāo)* (Own = m◦ *apnā*) اپنا کھانا کھاؤ

5. He has one thousand Rupees. *(us ke pāsa ek hazar rupaye haĩ)*

اس کے پاس ایک ہزار روپے ہیں

6. Sunīl is tall boy. *(Sunīl lambā laḍkā hai)* (Tall, long = m◦ *lambā*) سنیل لمبا لڑکا ہے

7. The clothes are wet. *(kapaḍe gīle haĩ)* कपड़े गीले हैं। Wet = m◦ *gīlā* کپڑے گیلے ہیں

8. My shirt is blue. *(merī kamīj nīlī hai)* (Blue = m◦ *nīlā*) میری قمیص نیلی ہے

9. You are tired. *āp thake haĩ. (√thak)* (Tired = m◦ *thakā*) آپ تھکے ہیں

10. The water is hot. *(pānī garam hai)* (hot = *garam*) پانی گرم ہے

11. It is true. *(yah sach hai)* यह सच है। (True = *sach*) یہ سچ ہے

12. The window is open. *(khiḍakī khulī hai)*-(Open = m◦ *khulā*, f◦ *khulī*) کھڑکی کھلی ہے

13. This job is small. *(yah kām chhoṭā hai)* (Small = m◦ *choṭā*) یہ کام چھوٹا ہے

14. I brought fresh fruit. *(maĩ tāje fal lāyā)* (Fresh = m◦ *tājā*) میں تازہ پھل لایا

15. He took a longer route. *(us ne lambā rāstā liyā)* (long = m◦ *lambā*) اسنے لمبا رستہ لیا

MORE ADJECTIVES TO LEARN

All *sab* (सब) سب

Bad *burā* (बुरा) برا

Beautiful *khūbsūrat* (खूबसूरत) خوبصورت

Big *baḍā* (बड़ा) بڑا

Bright *chamkīlā* (चमकीला) چمکیلا

Clean *sāf* (साफ़) صاف

Closed *band* (बंद) بند

Coarse, base *ghaṭiyā* (घटिया) گھٹیا

Cold *thaṇḍā* (ठंडा) ٹھنڈا	Cruel *zālim* (ज़ालिम) ظالم
Dead *murdā* (मुरदा) مردہ	Difficult *mushkil* (मुश्किल) مشکل
Dim, faint *dhūndalā* (धूंदला) دھندلا	Dirty *gandā* (गंदा) گندا
Dishonest *beīmān* (बे-ईमान) بے ایمان	Easy *āsān* (आसान) آسان
Empty *khālī* (खाली) خالی	False *jhūṭhā* (झूटा) جھوٹا
Fat *moṭa* (मोटा) موٹا	Foolish *bevakūf* (बेवकूफ़) بے وقوف
Free *āzād* (आज़ाद) آزاد	Fresh *tājā* (ताज़ा) تازہ
Gentle *sharif* (शरीफ़) شریف	Good *achchhā* (अच्छा) اچھا
Guilty *mujrim* (मुजरिम) مجرم	Handsome *khūbsūrat* (खूबसूरत) خوبصورت
Happy *khush* (खुश) خوش	Hard *kaḍā* (सख़्त) سخت
Heavy *bhārī* (भारी) بھاری	High *ūnchā* (ऊँचा) اونچا
Hot *garam* (गरम) گرم	Hot, warm *garam* (गरम) گرم
Humble *narm dil* (नर्म दिल) نرم دل	Ignorant *beilmī* (बेइल्मी) بے علمی
Innocent *masum* (मासूम) معصوم	Kind *raham dil* (रहम दिल) رحم دل
Large *baḍā* (बड़ा) بڑا	Lazy *kāhil* (काहिल) کاہل
Less *kam* (कम) (adv०) کم	Light *halakā* (हलका) ہلکا
Little *chhoṭā* (छोटा) چھوٹا	Long *lambā* (लंबा) لمبا
Low, base *nīchā* (नीचा) نیچا	More, much *zyādā* (ज़्यादा) زیادہ
Narow *tang* (क=तंग) تنگ	Old *būdhā* (बूढ़ा) بوڑھا
Open *khulā* (खुला) کھولا	Poor *garīb* (गरीब) غریب
Quick, sharp *tez* (तेज़) تیز	Rich *amīr* (अमीर) امیر
Sad *dukhī* (दुःखी) دکھی	Sharp, quick *tez* (तेज़) تیز

Slow *dhīre, āhistā* (धीरे, आहिस्ता دھیرے، آہستہ

Smart *hoshiyār* (होशियार) ہوشیار

Sorry *dukhī* (दुखी) دکھی

Stale *bāsā* (बासा) باسا

Superior *umda* (उमदा) عمدہ

Tall *lambā* (लंबा) لمبا

Timid *buzdil* (बुज़ दिल) بزدل

Ugly *badsūrat* (बद सूरत) بدصورت

Weak *kamjhor* (कमज़ोर) کمزور

Wise *aklmand* (अक्लमंद) عقلمند

Soft *mulāim* (मुलाइम) ملائم

Sour *khaṭṭā* (खट्टा) کھٹا

Strong *mazbūt* (मज़बूत) مضبوط

Sweet *mīṭhā* (मीठा) میٹھا

Thin *patalā* (पतला) پتلا

True *sachc* (सच) سچ

Warm, hot *garam* (गरम) گرم

Wild *janglī* (जंगली) جنگلی

Young *jawān* (जवान) جوان

All names of Numerals and Colours are Adjectives.

Remember : Colours have Genders (m. f.), the default is Masculine, singular.

For numerals, please see Lesson 2, *Introduction to Numerals.*

Red (*lāl*) लाल لال

Blue (*nīlā*) नीला نیلا

Black (*kālā*) काला کالا

Purple (*Jamnī*) जामनी جامنی

Pink (*gulābī*) गुलाबी گلابی

Green (*harā*) हरा ہرا

Yellow (*pīlā*) पीला پیلا

White (*safed*) सफेद سفید

Brown (*bhūrā*) भूरा بھورا

11.2 THE ADVERBS

DEFINITION : The word that qualifies a verb or an adjective is an Adverb.

RULE :

Adverbs do not have any gender, number, person, tense or case. They do not change with the verb or adjective they qualify, therefore, they are called INDECLINABLES.

EXERCISE *mashq* (مشق मश्क) **54** : Use of Adverbs

Translate the English sentences into Hindī (Answers are given for help)

1. Rānī walks fast. *(Rānī tez chaltī hai)* रानी तेज़ चलती है। رانی تیز چلتی ہے

2. He always helps. *(vah hameshā madad kartā hai)*

वह हमेशा मदद करता है। وہ ہمیشہ مدد کرتا ہے

3. Please move backward. *(barāha meherbānī pīchhe haṭo)*

बराह मेहरबानी पीछे हटो। براہ مہربانی پیچھے ہٹو (Please = *barāh meharbānī* براہ مہربانی)

4. I came before he did. *(maĩ us se pahale āyā)*

मैं उससे पहले आया। میں اس سے پہلے آیا

5. He wants money right now. *(us ko paise abhī chāhiye)*

उसको पैसे अभी चाहिये। اسکو پیسے ابھی چاہیے

6. Sunīl came here twice. *(Sunīl yahā̃ do bār āyā)*

सुनील यहाँ दो बार आया। سنیل یہاں دو بار آیا

7. She knows me well. *(vah muzay achchhī tarah se jānatī hai)*

वह मुझे अच्छी तरह से जानती है। وہ مجھے اچھی طرح سے جانتی ہے

8. This is better than that one. *(yah us se behatar hai)*

यह उससे बेहतर है। یہ اس سے بہتر ہے

9. Kindly give me ten dollars. *(barāhe karam muzay das dālar do)*

बराहे करम मुझे दस डॉलर दो। باره کرم مجھے دس دالر دو

10. Otherwise I will go. *(varanā mai̐ chal jāū̐ngā)*

वरना मैं चला जाऊँगा। ورنہ میں چلا جاونگا

11. Where is your friend? *(āp kā dost kahā̐ hai?)*

आपका दोस्त कहाँ है? آپکا دوست کہاں ہے؟

12. When did you hear this? *(āp ne yah kab sunā?)*

आपने यह कब सुना? آپ نے یہ کب سنا؟

13. Why are you sad? *(tum udās kyo̐ ho?)* तुम उदास क्यों हो? تم اداس کیوں ہو

14. How was this written? *(yah kaise likhā thā?)* यह कैसे लिखा था? یہ کیسے لکھا تھا

15. Speak slowly *(āhiṣtā bolo)* आहिश्ता बोलो। آہستہ بولو

16. Say it again. *(fir se kaho)* फिर से कहो। پھر سے کہو

17. Ali will not come now. *(Ali ab nahī̐ āyegā)*

अली अब नहीं आएगा। علی اب نہیں آئے گا

18. I like it very much. *(mai̐ ise bahut chāhatā hū̐, muzay yah bahut achchhā lagatā hai)* मैं इसे बहुत चाहता हूँ, मुझे यह बहुत अच्छा लगता है।

میں اسے بہت چاہتا ہوں، مجھے یہ بہت اچھا لگتا ہے

19. It is not very bad. *(yah bahut burā nahī̐ hai)*

यह बहुत बुरा नहीं है। یہ بہت برا نہیں ہے

20. He stood up at once. *(vah ekadam khaḍā huā)*

वह एकदम खड़ा हुआ। وہ ایک دم کھڑا ہوا

LESSON 12

GENERAL KNOWLEDGE AND VOCABULARY

INDEX

12.1 ANIMALS, Domastic घरेलु जानवर **Gharelu janvar** گھریلو جانور

12.2 ANIMALS, Wild जंगली जानवर **Jungli Janwar** جنگلی جانور

12.3 BIRDS परिंदे **Parinde** پرندے

12.4 BODY जिस्म **Jism** جسم

12.5 BODY CONDITIONS बीमारियाँ **Bimariyan** بیماریاں

12.6 BUSINESS सौदागरी **Kārobār** کاروبار

12.7 CITIES शहर **Shahar** شہر

12.8 CLOTHING etc. कपड़े Kapḍe کپڑے

12.9 COUNTRIES वतन **Vatan** وطن

12.10 DAYS OF THE WEEK सप्तह के दिन **Saptah ke din** ہفتے کے دن

12.11 FLOWERS फूल **Phool** پھول

12.12 FOOD STUFF खाने पीने का सामान **Khāne pīne ke samān** کھانے پینے کا سامان

12.13 FRUITS फल **Phal** پھل

12.14 HOUSEHOLD THINGS घरेलु सामान **Gharelu saman** گھریلو سامان

12.15 JEWELRY जवाहरात **Javāhrāt** جواہرات

12.16 METALS धातुएँ **Dhātuẽ** دھاتیں

12.17 MUSIC संगीत **Sangeet** سنگیت

12.18 NAMES OF CHRISTIAN PEOPLE

12.19 NAMES OF HINDU PEOPLE

12.20 NAMES OF MUSLIM PEOPLE

12.21 NAMES OF SIKH PEOPLE

12.22 PLANTS दरख्त **Darkht** درخت

12.23 PROFESSIONS पेशे और कारोबार **Peshe aur Kārobār** پیشےاورکاروبار

12.24 RELATIONS रिश्ते **Rishte** رشتے

12.25 SCHOOL स्कूल **Skool** مدرسہ

12.26 SPICES मसाले **Masale** مصالے

12.27 TOOLS आलात **Alāt** آلات

12.28 VEGETABLES सब्ज़ियाँ **Sabziyā̃** سبزیاں

12.29 WARFARE जंगी सामान Jungi Saman جنگی سامان

12.30 WORMS, INSECTS कीड़े मकोड़े kide Makode کیڑے مکوڑے

12.1 ANIMALS, Domastic घरेलु जानवर **Gharelu janvar** گھریلو جانور

Buffalo	भैंस	*bhains*	بھینس	Bull	सांड	*sānḍ*	ساںد
Calf	बछड़ा	*bachaḍā*	بچھڑا	Camel	ऊँट	*ūnṭ*	اوس
Cat	बिल्ली	*billī*	بلی	Cow	गाय	*gāy*	گائے
Dog	कुत्ता	*kuttā*	کںا	Donkey	गधा	*gadhā*	گدھا
Goat	बकरी	*bakrī*	بکری	Horse	घोड़ा	*ghoḍā*	گھورا
Mouse	चूहा	*chūhā*	حوہا	Mule	खच्चर	*khacchar*	حچر
Ox	बैल	*bail*	بیل	Pig	सुअर	*sūar*	سور
Pony	टट्टू	*ṭaṭṭu*	سو	Rabbit	खरगोश	*khargosh*	خرگوس
Ram	मेंढा	*menḍhā*	مینڈھا	Sheep	भेड़	*bheḍ*	بھیڑ

12.2 ANIMALS, Wild जंगली जानवर **Jungli Janwar** حسگلی جانور

Bear	भालू	*bhālū*	بھالو	Crab	केकड़ा	*kekḍā*	کیکڑا
Deer	हिरन	*hiran*	مرں	Elephant	हाथी	*hāthī*	ہاکھی
Fish	मछली	*machhlī*	مچھلی	Jackal	गीदड़	*gīdaḍ*	گیدر

Jackal	सियार	*siyār*	سیار	Lion	शेर	*sher*	شیر
Mongoose	नेवला	*neolā*	نیولا	Monkey	बंदर	*bandar*	بندر
Panther	चित्ता	*chittā*	چیتا	Porcupine	झूझ	*zhuzh*	ژوژ
Rhino	गेंडा	*genḍā*	گینڈا	Squirrel	गिलहरी	*gilharī*	گلہری
Stag	बारहसिंगा	*bārahsingā*	بارہ سنگھا	Tiger	शेर	*sher*	شیر
Turtle	कछुआ	*kachhuā*	کچھوا	Wolf	भेडिया	*bhediyā*	بھیڑیا

12.3 BIRDS परिंदे Parinde پرندے

Bat	चिमगादड़	*chimgādaḍ*	چمگادڑ	Cockoo	कोयल	*koyal*	کویل
Duck	बतख	*batakh*	بطخ	Eagle	चील	*chīl*	چیل
Hawk	बाज़	*bāz*	باز	Hen	मुर्गी	*murgī*	مرغی
Heron	बगुला	*bagulā*	بگلا	Sparrow	चिड़िया	*chiḍiyā*	چڑیا
Nightangle	बुलबुल	*bulbul*	بلبل	Owl	उल्लू	*ullū*	الو
Parrot	तोता	*totā*	طوطا	Peacock	मोर	*mor*	مور
Quail	बटेर	*baṭer*	بٹیر	Rooster	मुर्गा	*murgā*	مرغا
Crow	कौवा	*kawā*	کوا	Swan	हंस	*hamsa*	ہنس

12.4 BODY जिस्म Jism جسم

Ankle	टख़ना	*ṭakhnā*	ٹخنہ	Arm	बाज़ू	*bāzū*	بازو
Back	पीठ	*pīṭh*	پیٹھ	Beard	दाढ़ी	*dāḍhī*	داڑھی
Blood	खून	*khūn*	خون	Body	जिसम	*jisam*	جسم

Brain	दिमाग़	*dimāg*	دماغ	Calf	पिंडली	*piṇḍlī*	پنڈلی
Cheek	गाल	*gāl*	گال	Chest	सीना	*sīnā*	سینہ
Chin	ठुड्डी	*ṭhuḍḍī*	ٹھوڑی	Elbow	कुहनी	*kuhnī*	کہنی
Eye	आँख	*ānkh*	آنکھ	Eyebrows	भोहें	*bhohẽ*	بھوں
Face	चेहरा	*chehrā*	چہرہ	Finger	उँगली	*unglī*	انگلی
Fist	मुट्ठी	*muṭṭhī*	مٹھی	Foot	पैर	*pair*	پیر
Forehead	पेशानी	*peshānī*	پیشانی	Hair	बाल	*bāl*	بال
Hand	हाथ	*hāth*	ہاتھ	Head	सिर	*sir*	سر
Heart	दिल	*dil*	دل	Heel	एड़ी	*eḍī*	ایڑی
Intestine	आँत	*ānt*	آنت	Jaw	जबड़ा	*jabḍā*	جبڑا
Kidney	गुरदा	*gurdā*	گردہ	Soul	रुह	*ruh*	روح
Knee	घुटना	*ghuṭnā*	گھٹنا	Leg	टाँग	*ṭāng*	ٹانگ
Lip	होंट	*honṭ*	ہونٹ	Liver	कलेजा	*kalejā*	کلیجہ
Lung	फेफड़ा	*fefḍā*	پھیپھڑا	Moustaches	मुँछें	*mūnchhẽ*	مونچھیں
Mouth	मुँह	*munh*	منھ	Nail	नाखून	*nākhūn*	ناخن
Neck	गर्दन	*gardan*	گردن	Nerve	रग	*rag*	رگ
Nose	नाक	*nāk*	ناک	Palm	हथेली	*hathelī*	ہتھیلی
Rib	पसली	*paslī*	پسلی	Skin	खाल	*khāl*	کھال
Skull	खोपड़ी	*khopḍī*	کھوپڑی	Stomach	पेट	*peṭ*	پیٹ
Thigh	जाँघा	*jāngh*	جانگھ	Throat	गला	*galā*	گلا
Thumb	अंगूठा	*angūṭhā*	انگوٹھا	Tongue	ज़बान	*zabān*	زبان

Tooth	दाँत	*dānt*	دانت	Vein	रग	*rag*	رگ
Waist	कमर	*kamar*	کمر	Wrist	कलाई	*kalāī*	کلائی

12.5 BODY CONDITIONS बीमारियाँ Bimariyan بیماریاں

Asthma	दमा	*damā*	دمہ	Bald	गंज	*ganja*	گنجا
Blind	अंधाा	*andhā*	اندھا	Boil	फोड़ा	*foḍā*	پھوڑا
Breath	साँस	*sāns*	سانس	Constipation	क़बज़	*qbaz*	قبض
Cough	ख़ाँसी	*khānsī*	کھانسی	Crazy	पागल	*pāgal*	پاگل
Delivery	ज़च्चकी	*jacchkī*	زچگی	Diarrhoea	दस्त	*dast*	دست
Disease	बीमारी	*bīmārī*	بیماری	Dwarf	बोना	*bonā*	بونا
Fever	बुख़ार	*bukhār*	بخار	Frail	दुबलाा	*dublā*	دبلا
Giddiness	चक्कर	*chakkar*	چکر	Headache	सरदर्द	*sardard*	سردرد
Health	सहत	*sahat*	صحت	Hiccup	हिचकी	*hichkī*	ہچکی
Hurt	चोट	*choṭ*	چوٹ	Indigestion	बदहज़मी	*badhazmī*	بدہضمی
Itch	ख़ुजली	*khujlī*	کھجلی	Mad	पागल	*apāgal*	پاگل
Obesity	मोटापा	*moṭapa*	موٹاپا	Pain	दर्द	*dard*	درد
Pimple	फिंसी	*finsī*	پھنسی	Pimple	मुहासा	*muhāsā*	مہاسہ
Pus	पीप	*pīp*	پیپ	Saliva	राल	*rāl*	رال
Sick	बीमार	*bīmār*	بیمار	Sleep	नींद	*nind*	نیند
Sneeze	छींक	*chhink*	چھینک	Sprain	मोच	*moch*	موچ
Stool	पाख़ाना	*pākhānā*	پاخانہ	Sweat	पसीना	*pasīnā*	پسینہ
Tears	आँसू	*ānsū*	آنسو	Thirst	प्यास	*pyās*	پیاس

Urine	पैशाब	*pashāb*	مساب	Voice	आवाज़	*āvāz*	آواز
Vomit	कै	*qai*	قے	Wound	ज़ख़म	*zakham*	زخم
Yawn	जमाही	*jamāhī*	جمای				

12.6 BUSINESS सौदागरी Kārobār کاروبار

Account	हिसाब	*hisāb*	حساب	Ankle	टख़ना	*ṭakhnā*	ٹخنہ
Average	औसत	*ausat*	اوسط	Balance	बाक़ी	*bāqī*	باقی
Bankruptsy	दिवाला	*diwālā*	دیوالیہ	Cash	नक़द	*naqad*	نقد
Charge	ख़र्चा	*kharchā*	خرچہ	Credit	उधार	*udhār*	ادھار
Current	जारी	*jārī*	جاری	Deposit	जमा	*jamā*	جمع
Distance	फ़ासला	*fāslā*	فاصلہ	Earning	आमदनी	*āmdaniī*	آمدنی
Economy	किफ़ाइत	*kifāit*	معیشت	Factory	कारख़ना	*karkhānā*	کارخانہ
Gap	फ़ासला	*fāslā*	فاصلہ	Income	आमदनी	*āmdanī*	آمدنی
Insurance	बीमा	*bīmā*	بیمہ	Job	काम	*kām*	کام
Letter	ख़त	*khat*	خط	Loan	क़रज़	*qara*	قرض
Loss	नुक़सान	*nuksān*	نقصان	Market	बाज़र	*bāzār*	بازار
Money	पैसे	*paise*	پیسے	Mrechant	सौदागर	*saudāgar*	سوداگر
Pay (to)	अदा	*adā*	ادا	Pay	तनख़्वाह	*tankhwāh*	تنخواہ
Price	क़ीमत	*qimat*	قیمت	Profit	मुनाफ़ा	*munāfā*	منافع
Sale	बिक्री	*bikrī*	بیکری	Saving	बचत	*bachat*	بچت
Treasury	ख़जाना	*khāzānā*	خزانہ	Work	काम	*kām*	کام

12.7 CITIES शहर **Shahar** شہر

Agra	आग्रा	*āgrā*	آگرہ	Amritsar	अमृतसर	*amritsar*	امرتسر
Ayodhya	अयोध्या	*ayodhyā*	ایودھیا	Bannu	बन्नू	*bannū*	بنو
Benaras	बनारस	*banāras*	بنارس	Bombay	मुंबई	*mumbaī*	مومبائی
Calcutta	कोलकता	*kolkatā*	کولکتہ	Delhi	दिल्ली	*dillī*	دلّی
Gaya	गया	*gayā*	گیا	Howrah	हावड़ा	*hāwḍā*	ہاورہ
Hyderabad	हैदराबाद	*haidrābād*	حیدرآباد	Islamabad	इस्लामाबाद	*islāmābād*	اسلام آباد
Jaipur	जयपुर	*jaipur*	جے پور	Kanpur	कानपुर	*kānpur*	کانپور
Karachi	कराची	*karāchī*	کراچی	Lahore	लाहोर	*lāhor*	لاہور
Lucknow	लखनऊ	*lakhnau*	لکھنو	Mathura	मथुरा	*mathurā*	متھرا
Merath	मेरठ	*meraṭh*	میرٹھ	Nagpur	नागपुर	*nāgpur*	ناگپور
Patna	पटना	*paṭnā*	پٹنہ	Peshawar	पेशावर	*peshāwar*	پشاور
Poona	पुणे	*puṇe*	پونے	Shimla	शिमला	*shimlā*	شملہ
Surat	सूरत	*sūrt*	سورت				

12.8 CLOTHING etc. कपड़े Kapḍe کپڑے

Belt	कमरबंद	*kamarband*	کمربند	Blanket	कम्बल	*kambal*	کمبل
Cap	टोपी	*ṭopī*	ٹوپی	Cloth	कपड़ा	*kapḍā*	کپڑا
Cotton	रूई	*rūī*	روئی	Gloves	दस्ताने	*dastāne*	دستانے
Hat	टोपी	*ṭopī*	ٹوپی	Lace	फ़ीता	*fītā*	فیتہ
Mattress	गद्दा	*gaddā*	گدا	Pants	पतलून	*patlūn*	پتلون
Pocket	जेब	*jeb*	جیب	Quilt	रजाई	*rajāī*	رضائی
Scarf	दुपट्टा	*dupaṭṭa*	دوپٹہ	Sheet	चादर	*chādar*	چادر

Shirt	क़मीज़	*qamīz*	قمیص	Silk	रेशिम	*reshim*	ریشم
Skirt	घाघरा	*ghāgharā*	گھاگھرا	Sleeve	आस्तिन	*āstin*	آستین
Sock	मोज़ा	*mozā*	موزہ	Towel	तौलिया	*tauliyā*	تولیہ
Turban	पगड़ी	*pagḍī*	پگڑی	Underwear	जांघिया	*jānghiyā*	جانگیہ
Uniform	वरदी	*vardī*	وردی	Veil	घूँघट	*ghūnghaṭ*	گھونگھٹ
Velvet	मख़मल	*makhmal*	مخمل				

12.9 COUNTRIES वतन Vatan وطن

America	अमरीका	*amrikā*	امریکہ	Arabia	अरब	*arab*	عرب
Chinā	चीन	*chīn*	چین	Ejypt	मिस्त्र	*misr*	مصر
England	इंग्लैंड	*ingland*	انگلینڈ	France	फ्राँस	*frāns*	فرانس
India	हिंदुस्तान	*hindustān*	ہندوستان	Iran	इरान	*irān*	ایران
Itali	इटली	*itlī*	اٹلی	Japan	जापान	*jāpān*	جاپان
Pakistan	पाकिस्तान	*pakistān*	پاکستان	Russiā	रूस	*rūs*	روس
Turky	तुर्की	*turkī*	ترکی				

12.10 DAYS OF THE WEEK सप्तह के दिन Saptah ke din ہفتہ کے دن

Sunday	इतवार	*itvār*	اتوار	Monday	सोमवार	*pīr*	پیر
Tuesday	मंगल	*mangal*	منگل	Wednesday	बुध	*budha*	بدھ
Thursday	जुमेरात	*jumerāt*	جمعرات	Friday	जुमा	*juma*	جمعہ
Saturday	शनिचर	*shanichar*	سنیچر				

12.11 FLOWERS फूल Phool پھول

Jasmine	चंबेली	*chambelī*	چمبلی	Lotus	कँवल	*kav̐al*	کنول
Marigold	गेंदा	*gendā*	گیندا	Rose	गुलाब	*gulāb*	گلاب
Sunflower	सूरजमुखी	*sūrajmukhī*	سورج مکھی				

12.12 FOOD STUFF खाने पीने का सामान Khāne pīne ke samān کھانے پینے کا سامان

Bread	चपाती	*chapātī*	چپاتی	Bread	रोटी	*roṭī*	روٹی
Butter	मक्खन	*makkhan*	مکھن	Cheese	पनीर	*panīr*	پنیر
Chickpea	चना	*chanā*	چنا	Corn	मकई	*makaī*	مکئی
Cream	मलाई	*malāī*	ملائی	Flour	आटा	*tāṭā*	آٹا
Food	खाना	*khānā*	کھانا	Grain	अनाज़	*anāz*	اناج
Honey	शहद	*shahad*	شہد	Ice	बरफ़	*baraf*	برف
Ice-cream	कुलफ़ी	*qulfī*	قلفی	Lentil	मसूर	*masūr*	مسور
Meat	गोश्त	*gosht*	گوشت	Milk	दूध	*dūdh*	دودھ
Mustard	राई	*rāī*	رائی	Oil	तेल	*tel*	تیل
Paddy	धान	*dhān*	دھان	Pea	मटर	*maṭar*	مٹر
Pickle	अचार	*achār*	اچار	Pulse	दाल	*dāl*	دال
Rice	चावल	*chaval*	چاول	Seasum	तिल	*til*	تل
Sugar	शक्कर	*shakkar*	شکر	Syrup	शरबत	*sharbat*	شربت
Tea	चाय	*chāy*	چائے	Vegetable	तरकारी	*tarkārī*	ترکاری
Vegetable	सब्ज़ी	*sabzī*	سبزی	Vinegar	सिरका	*sirkā*	سرکہ
Wheat	गंदम	*gandam*	گندم	Wine	शराब	*sharāb*	شراب
Yougrt	दही	*dahī*	دہی				

12.13 FRUITS फल Phal پھل

Banana	केला	*kelā*	کیلا	Guava	अमरूद	*amrūd*	امرود
Date	खजूर	*khajaūr*	کھجور	Fig	अंजीर	*anjīr*	انجیر
Grape	अंगूर	*angūr*	انگور	Mango	आम	*ām*	آم
Orange	नारंजी	*nāranjī*	نارنگی	Papaya	पपिता	*papitā*	پپیتا
Peach	आड़ू	*āḍū*	آڑو	Pineapple	अननास	*ananās*	اناناس
Plum	आलूचा	*ālūchā*	آلوچہ	Pomegranate	अनार	*anār*	انار
Tamarind	इमली	*imlī*	املی				

12.14 HOUSEHOLD THINGS घरेलु सामान Gharelu saman گھریلوساماں

Ash	राख	*rākh*	راکھ	Basket	टोकरी	*ṭokrī*	ٹوکری
Bowl	डोंगा	*ḍongā*	ڈونگا	Box	डब्बा	*ḍabbā*	ڈبہ
Broom	झाड़ू	*jhāḍū*	جھاڑو	Candle	मोमबती	*mombattī*	موم بتی
Chair	कुरसी	*kursī*	کرسی	Comb	कंघी	*kanghī*	کنگھی
Cot	चारपाई	*chārpāī*	چارپائی	Cup	प्याला	*pyālā*	پیالہ
Fork	कांटा	*kānṭā*	کانٹا	Fuel	ईंधन	*indhan*	ایندھن
Glass	गलास	*galās*	گلاس	Key	चाबी	*chābī*	چابی
Lamp	दीया	*dīyā*	دیا	Lock	ताला	*tālā*	تالا
Mat	चटाई	*chaṭāī*	چٹائی	Mesh	जाली	*jālī*	جالی
Mirror	आइना	*āinā*	آئینہ	Needle	सूई	*sūī*	سوئی
Oven	तंदूर	*tandūr*	تندور	Pillow	तकिया	*takiyā*	تکیہ

Plate	थाली	*thālī*	تھالی	Pot	बरतन	*bartan*	رتن
Rolling pin	बेलन	*belan*	بیلن	Sieve	छलनी	*chhalnī*	چھلنی
Soap	साबुन	*sābun*	صابن	Spoon	चमचा	*chamchā*	چمچہ
Stove	अंगीठी	*angīṭhī*	انگیٹھی	Stove	चूल्हा	*chūlhā*	چولہا
String	रस्सी	*rassī*	رسّی	Swing	झूला	*jhūlā*	جھولا
Table	मेज़	*mez*	میز	Tap	नल	*nal*	نل
Thread	धागा	*dhāgā*	دھاگا	Umbrella	छतरी	*chhatrī*	چھتری

12.15 JEWELRY जवाहरात Javāhrāt جواہرات

Anklet	पाज़ेब	*pāzeb*	باریب	Armlet	बाज़ूबंद	*bāzūband*	باروبند
Bangle	चूडी	*chūḍī*	چوری	Chain link	कड़ी	*kaḍī*	کری
Clip	चिमटी	*chimṭī*	چمٹی	Coral	मूँगा	*mūngā*	مونگا
Diamond	हीरा	*hīrā*	سرا	Earring	काँटा	*kānṭā*	کانٹا
Emerlad	पन्ना	*pannā*	سا	Garland	माला	*mālā*	مالا
Gold	सोना	*sonā*	سوبا	Head-locket	टीका	*ṭīkā*	ٹیکا
Jewellery	जेवरात	*jewarāt*	زورات	Necklace	हार	*hār*	ہار
Nose-pin	लोंग	*laung*	لونگ	Nose-ring	नथ	*nath*	نتھ
Opal	दुधिया	*dudhiyā*	دوودھیا	Pearl	मोती	*motī*	موتی
Quartz	बिल्लोर	*billor*	بلّور	Ring	अंगूठी	*angūṭhī*	انگوکھی
Ruby	लाल	*lāl*	لال	Sapphire	नीलम	*nīlam*	نیلم
Silver	चाँदी	*chāndī*	چاندی	Tiara	ताज़	*ṭāz*	ماج
Turquoise	फ़िरोज़ा	*firozā*	فیرورہ	Wristlet	कंगन	*kamgan*	کنگن

12.16 METALS धातुएँ Dhātuẽ دھاتیں

Brass	पीतल	*pītal*	پیتل	Copper	तांबा	*tāmbā*	تانبا
Gold	सोना	*sonā*	سونا	Iron	लोहा	*lohā*	لوہا
Lead	सीसा	*sīsā*	سیسہ	Mercury	पारा	*pārā*	پارا
Silver	चाँदी	*chāndī*	چاندی	Tin	रांगा	*rāngā*	رانگہ
Zink	जस्त	*jast*	جست				

12.17 MUSIC संगीत Sangeet سنگیت

Bell	घंटी	*ghanṭī*	گھنٹی	Bugle	बिगुल	*bugul*	بیگول
Clarionet	शहनाई	*shahnāī*	شہنائی	Conch	शंख	*shankh*	سنکھ
Cymbal	झाँझ	*jhānjh*	جھانجھ	Drumet	डुगडुगी	*ḍugḍugī*	ڈگڈگی
Drums	तबला	*tablā*	طبلہ	Flute	बाँसुरी	*bānsurī*	بانسری
Guitar (ind.)	सितार	*sitār*	ستار	Harminium	बाजा	*bājā*	باجا
Harp	सारंगी	*sārangī*	سارنگی	Kettledrum	नक़ारा	*naqārā*	نقارہ
Organ	बाजा	*bājā*	باجا	Playing	बजाना	*bajānā*	بجانا
Song	गाना	*gānā*	گانا	Tabor	तबला	*tablā*	طبلہ
Tambourine	डफ़	*daf*	دف	Tomtom	ढोलक	*ḍholak*	ڈھولک
Violin	बेला	*belā*	بیلا	Whistle	सीटी	*sīṭī*	سیٹی

12.18 NAMES OF CHRISTIAN PEOPLE

Betty	बेटी	*beṭī*	بیٹی	Bob	बोब	*bob*	بوب
Carol	केरोल	*kerol*	کیرول	Cathey	कैथी	*kethi*	کیتھی
Dan	डान	*dan*	ڈان	Dany	डैनी	*denī*	ڈینی
David	डेवीड	*ḍeviḍ*	ڈیوڈ	Frank	फ्रैंक	*frank*	فرینک

George	जोर्ज	*jorj*	جارج	John	जौन	*jon*	جون
Julie	जूली	*jūlī*	جولی	Ken	केन	*ken*	کین
Linda	लिंडा	*liṇḍā*	لنڈا	Nancy	नेन्सी	*nensī*	نینسی
Neil	नील	*nīl*	نیل	Paul	पाल	*pāl*	پال
Peter	पीटर	*pīṭar*	پیٹر	Roger	रोजर	*rojar*	روجر
Sam	सैम	*sam*	سیم	Terry	टेरी	*ṭerī*	ٹیری

12.19 NAMES OF HINDU PEOPLE

Anil	अनील	*anīl*	انیل	Anita	अनिता	*anitā*	انیتا
Arun	अरुण	*aruṇ*	اروں	Aruna	अरुणा	*aruṇā*	اروںا
Bimla	बिमला	*bimlā*	بملا	Dev	देव	*dev*	دیو
Gopal	गोपाल	*gopāl*	گوپال	Jagdish	जगदीश	*jagdīsh*	جگدیش
Kamala	कमला	*kamlā*	کملا	Krishan	क्रिशन	*krishan*	کرشن
Kumar	कुमार	*kumār*	کمار	Mala	माला	*mālā*	مالا
Parkash	परकाश	*parkash*	پرکاش	Radha	राधा	*rādhā*	رادھا
Raj	राज	*rāj*	راج	Ramesh	रमेश	*ramesh*	رمیش
Ramlāl	रामलाल	*rāmlāl*	رام لال	Seeta	सीता	*sītā*	سیتا
Shashi	शशी	*shashī*	ششی	Shivrām	शिवराम	*shivrām*	شیورام
Shyam	श्याम	*shyām*	شیام	Subhash	सुभाष	*subhāsh*	سبھاش
Sudhir	सुधीर	*sudhīr*	سودھیر	Sunil	सुनील	*sunil*	سنیل
Sunita	सुनीता	*sunītā*	سنیتا	Surinder	सुरेंदर	*surendar*	سریندر

12.20 NAMES OF MUSLIM PEOPLE

Ahmad	अहमद	*ahmad*	احمد	Ajij	अज़ीज़	*azīz*	عزیز
Aziza	अज़ीज़ा	*azīzā*	عزیزہ	Ali	अली	*alī*	علی
Anwar	अनवर	*anvar*	انور	Aslam	असलम	*aslam*	اسلم
Begam	बेगम	*begam*	بیگم	Fatima	फ़ात्मा	*fatmā*	فاطمہ
Husna-ara	हुस्नआरा	*husnaārāhhāl*	حسن آرا	Jamil	जमील	*jamīl*	جمیل
Khalik	ख़लीक़	*khalīq*	خلیق	Mia	मीयाँ	*mian*	میاں
Muhammad	मुहम्मद	*muhammad*	محمد	Mumtaz	मुमताज़	*mumtāz*	ممتاز
Nabī	नबी	*nabī*	نبی	Nasim	नसीम	*nasīm*	نسیم
Nasima	नसीमा	*nasīmā*	نسیمہ	Nausha	नौशा	*naushāl*	نوشہ
Rais	रईस	*rais*	رئیس	Shamima	शमीमा	*shamīmā*	شمیمہ
Sharif	शरीफ़	*sharīf*	شریف	Sherkhān	शेरखाँ	*sherkhā̃*	شیرخاں

12.21 NAMES OF SIKH PEOPLE

Banta	बंता	*bantā*	بنتا	Manmohan	मनमोहन	*manmohan*	منموہن
Gurtek	गुरटेक	*gurṭek*	گرٹیک	Singh	सिंग	*singh*	سنگھ
Kaur	कौर	*kaur*	کور	Gobind	गोबिंद	*gobind*	گوبند
Gurnām	गुरनाम	*gurnām*	گورنام	Santokh	संतोख	*santoka*	سنتوکھ
Milkha	मिलखा	*milkhā*	ملکھا	Ranjit	रणजीत	*raṇjīt*	رنجیت
Nanak	नानक	*nānak*	نانک	Santa	संता	*santā*	سنتا

12.22 PLANTS दरख्त Darkht درخت

Bark	छाल	*chhāl*	چھال	Branch	टहनी	*ṭahanī*	ٹہنی
Bud	कली	*kalī*	کلی	Bulb	माँसल जड़	*mā̃sal jaḍ*	ماسل جڑ

Gum	गोंद	*gond*	گوند	Juice	रस	*ras*	رس
Leaf	पत्ती	*pattī*	ی	Peel	छिलका	*chhilkā*	چھلکا
Root	जड़ा	*jaḍ*	جڑ	Seed	बीज	*bīj*	بیج
Stem	तना	*tanā*	تنا	Stone	गुठली	*guṭhlī*	گٹھلی
Thorn	काँटा	*kānṭā*	کانٹا	Wood	लकड़ी	*lakḍī*	لکڑی
Bamboo	बाँस	*bāns*	مانس	Banyan	बरगद	*bargad*	رگد
Flower	फूल	*fūl*	پھول	Guava	अमरूद	*amrūd*	امرود
Mango	आम	*ām*	آم	alm	ताड़	*tāḍ*	مار
Pine	चीड़	*chīḍ*	چیڑ	Teak	सागवन	*sāgwan*	ساگون
Grass	घास	*ghās*	گھاس				

12.23 PROFESSIONS पेशे और कारोबार Peshe aur Kārobār پیشے اور کاروبار

Advocate	वकील	*wakil*	وکیل	Agent	दलाल	*dalāl*	دلال
Barber	हजाम	*hajām*	حجام	Broker	दलाल	*dalāl*	دلال
Butcher	कसाई	*kasāī*	قصای	Carpenter	बढ़ई	*baḍhaī*	رھئی
Cashier	ख़जांची	*khajānchī*	خزانچی	Cobbler	मोची	*mochī*	موحی
Confectioner	हलवाई	*halwaī*	حلوائی	Contractor	ठेकेदार	*ṭhekedār*	ٹھیکے دار
Cook	बावरची	*bāvarchī*	ماورحی	Doctor	हकीम	*hakīm*	حکیم
Farmer	किसान	*kisān*	کساں	Gardener	माली	*mālī*	مالی
Guard	दरबान	*darbān*	درمان	Jeweller	जौहरी	*jauharī*	جوہری
Landlord	जागिरदार	*jāgirdār*	حاگردار	Magician	जादूगर	*jādūgar*	جادوگر
Mason	राज	*rāj*	راح	Milkman	ग्वाला	*gwālā*	گوالا
Nurse	दाई	*dāī*	دائی	Worker	मज़दूर	*mazdūr*	مزدور

Peon	चपरासी	*chaprāsī*	چپراسی	Poet	शायर	*shāyar*	شاعر
Police	सिपाही	*sipāhī*	سپاہی	Politician	सियासतदान	*siyāsatdān*	سیاستدان
Postman	डाकीया	*ḍakīyā*	ڈاکیا	Priest	पाद्री	*pādrī*	پادری
shopkeeper	दुकानदार	*dukāndār*	دکاندار	Surgeon	जर्राह	*jarrāh*	جراح
Tailor	दर्ज़ी	*darzī*	درزی	Teacher	उस्ताद	*ustād*	استاد
Treasurer	ख़जांची	*khajānchī*	خزانچی	Washerman	धोबी	*dhobī*	دھوبی
Weaver	जुलाहा	*julāhā*	جلاہا				

12.24 RELATIONS रिश्ते Rishte رشتے

Aunt	चाची	*chachī*	چچی	Brother	भाई	*bhāī*	بھائی
Brother' son	भतीजा	*bhatījā*	بھتیجا	Brother's daughter	भतीजी	*bhatījī*	بھتیجی
Brother's wife	भाभी	*bhābhī*	بھابھی	Daughter	बेटी	*beṭī*	بیٹی
Daughter-in-law	बहू	*bahū*	بہو	Family	ख़ानदान	*khāndān*	خاندان
Father	बाप	*bāp*	باپ	Father-in-law	सुसर	*susar*	سسر
Father's brother	चचा	*chachā*	چچا	Father's father	दादा	*dādā*	دادا
Father's mother	दादी	*dādī*	دادی	Father's sister	फूफी	*fūfī*	پھوپھی
Friend	दोस्त	*dost*	دوست	Grandson	नवासा	*navāsā*	نواسا
Granddaughter	नवासी	*navāsī*	نواسی	Heair	वारिस	*wāris*	وارث
Husband	शौहर	*shauhar*	شوہر	Husband's brother	देवर	*devar*	دیور
Husband's sister	ननद	*nanad*	نند	Love	मुहब्बत	*muhabbat*	محبت
Mother	माँ	*mā̃*	ماں	Mother-in-law	सास	*sās*	ساس
Mother's brother	मामूँ	*māmū̃*	ماموں	Mother's brother's wife	मामी	*māmī*	مامی

Mother's father	नाना	*nānā*	نانا	Mother's mother	नानी	*nānī*	نانی
Mother's sister	खाला	*khālā*	خالہ	Neighbor	पड़ोसी	*paḍosī*	پڑوسی
Own	अपना	*apanā*	اپنا	Relative	रिश्तेदार	*rishtedār*	رشتہ دار
Sister	बहन	*bahan*	بہن	Sister's daughter	भाँजी	*bhā̃ñjī*	بھانجی
Sister's husband	बहनोई	*bahanoī*	بہنوئی	Sister's son	भाँजा	*bhā̃ñjā*	بھانجہ
Son	बेटा	*beṭā*	بیٹا	Son-in-law	दामाद	*dāmād*	داماد
Step xx	सौतेला–	*sautelā-*	سوتیلا	Stranger	परदेसी	*paradesī*	پردیسی
Wife	बीवी	*bīvī*	بیوی	Wife's brother	साला	*sālā*	سالا
Wife's sister	साली	*sālī*	سالی				

12.25 SCHOOL स्कूल Skool مدرسہ

Bench	चौकी	*chaukī*	چوکی	Dictionary	लुघत	*lughat*	لغت
Envelop	लिफ़ाफ़ा	*lifāfā*	لفافہ	Eraser	रबड़	*rabaḍ*	ربڑ
Glue	गोंद	*gond*	گوند	Ground	मैदान	*maidān*	میداں
Ink	स्याही	*syahī*	سیاہی	Inkpot	दवात	*davāt*	دوات
Map	नक्शा	*nakshā*	نقشہ	Paper	काग़ज़	*kāgaz*	کاغذ
Pen	क़लम	*kalam*	قلم	Pupil	शागिर्द	*shāgird*	شاگرد
Room	कमरा	*kamrā*	کمرہ	Study	पढ़ाई	*paḍhāī*	پڑھائی
Table	मेज़	*mez*	میز	Lace	फ़ीता	*fītā*	فیتا
Teacher	उस्ताद	*ustād*	استاد				

12.26 SPICES मसाले Masale مصالے

Aniseed	सौंफ़	*saunf*	سونف	Asafoetida	हिंग	*hing*	ہینگ
Basil	तुलसी	*tulsī*	تلسی	Cardamom	इलाची	*ilāchī*	الاچی
Cinnamon	दारचीनी	*dārchīnī*	دارچینی	Coriander	धनिया	*dhaniyā*	دھنیا
Cumin	जीरा	*jīrā*	جیرا	Ginger	अद्रक	*adrak*	ادرک
Linseed	अलसी	*alsī*	السی	Nutmeg	जायफल	*jāyfal*	جائفل
Pepper	मिर्च	*mirch*	مرچ	Tamarind	इमली	*imlī*	املی
Turmeric	हलदी	*haldī*	ہلدی	Walnut	अख़रोट	*akhroṭ*	اخروٹ

12.27 TOOLS आलात Alāt آلات

Axe	गैती	*gaitī*	گیتی	Chisel	छेनी	*chhenī*	چھینی
File	रेती	*retī*	ریتی	Hammer	हथौड़ा	*hathauḍā*	ہتھوڑا
Plough	हल	*hal*	ہل	Saw	आरी	*ārī*	آری
Scissors	कैंची	*qainchī*	قینچی	Screwdriver	पेंचकस	*penchkas*	پیچ کس
Spade	फावड़ा	*fāvaḍā*	پھاوڑا	Syringe	पिचकारी	*pichkārī*	پچکاری

12.28 VEGETABLES सब्ज़ियाँ Sabziyā̃ سبزیاں

Cabbage	बंदगोभी	*bandgobhī*	بند گوبھی	Carrot	गाजर	*gājar*	گاجر
Chilli	मिर्च	*mirch*	مرچ	Cocoanut	नारियल	*nāriyal*	ناریل
Eggplant	बैंगन	*baingan*	بینگن	Jackfruit	कठल	*kathal*	کٹھل
Lemon	लीमू	*līmū*	لیمو	Lotus	कँवल	*kaval*	کنول
Okra	भिंडी	*bhinḍī*	بھنڈی	Pea	मटर	*maṭar*	مٹر
Potato	आलू	*ālū*	آلو	Pumpkin	कद्दू	*kaddū*	کدو
Raddish	मूली	*mūlī*	مولی	Spinach	पालक	*pālak*	پالک

Sugarcane	गन्ना	*gannā*	گنا	Turnip	शलग़म	*shalgam*	شلغم

12.29 WARFARE जंगी सामान Jungi Saman جنگی سامان

Army	फौज	*fauj*	فوج	Submarine	आबलुज़		آبدور
Attack	हमला	*hamlā*	حملہ	Battle	लड़ाई	*laḍāī*	لڑائی
Bomb	बम	*bam*	بم	Bullet	गोली	*golī*	گولی
Cannon	तोप	*top*	توپ	Cartridge	कारतुस	*kārtus*	کارتوس
Defence	बचाव	*bachāo*	بچاو	Enemy	दुश्मन	*dushman*	دشمن
Gunpowder	बारूद	*bārūd*	بارود	Ship	जहाज़	*jahaz*	جہاز
Submarine	आबदोज़	*ābdoz*	آبدور	Treaty	सुलह	*sulah*	صلح
Trench	खंदक़	*khandaq*	خندق				

12.30 WORMS, INSECTS कीड़े मकोड़े kide Makode کیڑے مکوڑے

Alligator	मगरमछ	*magarmachh*	مگرمچھ	Bee	मक्खी	*makkhī*	مکھی
Butterfly	तितली	*titlī*	تتلی	Crab	केलड़ा	*kekḍā*	ککڑے
Cricket	झिंगुर	*jhingur*	جھنگور	Flea	पिसू	*pisū*	پسو
Fly	मक्खी	*makkhī*	مکھی	Frog	मेंढक	*menḍhak*	مینڈک
Glow worm	जुगनु	*jugnu*	جگنو	Leech	जोंक	*jonk*	جونک
Louse	जों	*jõ*	جوں	Lizard	छिपकली	*chhipkalī*	چھپکلی
Lobster	झिंगा	*jhingā*	جھینگا	Locust	टिड्डी	*ṭiḍḍī*	ٹڈی
Poison	ज़हर	*zahar*	زہر	Scorpion	बिच्छू	*bichhū*	بچھو
Snake	साँप	*sānp*	سانپ	Termite	दिमक	*dimak*	دیمک

COMMON URDU VERBS

* = Transitive verb, (The actions that need an Object)

agree	مان	*mān*	fly*	اڑا	*uḍā*	rub*	مل	*mal*
arrange*	رکھ	*rakh*	forget*	بھول	*bhūl*	run	بھاگ	*bhāg*
become	ہو	*ho*	fry*	تل	*tal*	say*	کہ	*kah*
bother*	ستا	*satā*	get	مل	*mil*	scare*	ڈرا	*ḍarā*
break	ٹوٹ	*ṭūṭ*	give*	دے	*de*	sell*	بیچ	*bech*
break*	توڑ	*toḍ*	go	جا	*jā*	sew*	سی	*sī*
bring*	لا	*lā*	hear	سن	*sun*	sieve*	چھان	*chhān*
burn	جل	*jal*	hide	چھپ	*chhip*	sing*	گا	*gā*
burn*	جلا	*jalā*	hide*	چھپا	*chhipā*	sleep	سو	*so*
call*	بلا	*bulā*	kill*	مار	*mār*	sow*	بو	*bo*
can	سک	*sak*	know*	جان	*jān*	speak	بول	*bol*
carry	ڈھو	*ḍho*	leak	بہ	*bah*	see	دیکھ	*dekh*
celebrate*	منا	*manā*	lick*	چاٹ	*chāṭ*	stay, live	رہ	*rah*
come	آ	*ā*	like*	چاہ	*chāh*	steal*	چرا	*churā*
cook*	پکا	*pakā*	live (be alive)	جی	*jī*	sulk	روٹھ	*rūṭh*
cry	رو	*ro*	loose*	کھو	*kho*	take*	لے	*le*
cut*	کاٹ	*kāṭ*	make*	بنا	*banā*	teach*	پڑھا	*paḍhā*
die	مر	*mar*	meet	مل	*mil*	tell*	بتا	*batā*
dig*	کھود	*khod*	mix*	ملا	*milā*	touch*	چھو	*chhoo*
do*	کر	*kar*	move	ہل	*hil*	walk	چل	*chal*
drink*	پی	*pī*	move*	ہلا	*hilā*	want*	چاہ	*chāh*
drive	چلا	*chalā*	open	کھل	*khul*	wash*	دھو	*dho*
drop*	گرا	*girā*	open*	کھول	*khol*	weigh*	تول	*tol*
eat*	کھا	*khā*	peel*	چھیل	*chhīl*	win*	جیت	*jīt*
fall	گر	*gir*	read*	پڑھ	*paḍh*	write*	لکھ	*likh*
fear	ڈر	*ḍar*	rip*	چیر	*chīr*			
fly	اڑ	*uḍ*	rob*	لوٹ	*lūṭ*			

NOTE : The underlined four are most important action words required for making sentences.

LESSON 13

URDU CONVERSATIONAL ROADMAP

(A) ASKING, ANSWERING and EXPRESSING

13.1 Begin with Greetings

<u>How to say hello!</u> **Interjection:** ***aadaab, namaste ji, namaste, kya hal hai?...etc.***

*** Hello! *(ādab!)* آداب** *** Hello! Goodmorning *(ādab arj hai!)* آداب عرض ہے**

*** How are you *(āp kaise hai̐?)* آپ کیسے ہیں *(tum kaise ho?)* تم کیسے ہو**

<u>Replying the greeting</u> **Adj.: *achha;* 1st Person Pronoun: *mai;* Verb: *hoon***

*** I am fine *(mai̐ ṭhīk hū̐)* میں ٹھیک ہوں *(mai̐ achhā hū̐)* میں اچھا ہوں**

<u>Appreciation</u> **Interjection: *shukriya.* Goodnight, Good bye etc.**

*** Thank you! *(shukriyā!)* شکریہ** *** Good night! (*shab-b-khair!*) (شب بخیر)**

*** Good bye! (*ijāzat dījiye*) اجازت دیجئے (*alvidā!*) الوداع (*khudā haifij*) خداحافظ**

13.2 Introducing yourself

<u>Asking one's name</u> **Interrogative: *'kya?'* Possessive Pronoun: *'aap ka'***

*** <u>What</u> is your name? *(āpakā nām <u>kyā</u> hai?)* آپ کا نام کیا ہے؟**

*** <u>My</u> name is Paul *(<u>merā</u> nām Pāl hai)* میرا نام پال ہے**

<u>Giving compliment</u> **Expression : *'bahut achha;'* Nouns : *naam;* Verb: *hai***

*** Your name is very nice. (*āpa ka nām bahut achha hai*) آپ کا نام بہت اچھا ہے**

13.3 Learning by asking

<u>Asking where one lives?</u> **Adv.: *kahaan;* Habitual Present Tense verb: *rahnaa***

*** <u>Where</u> do you live? *(āp <u>kahā̐</u> rahate hai̐?)* آپ کہاں رہتے ہیں؟**

<u>Telling where you live</u> **Listening their reply and remembering it to form your answer.**

*** I live in Kanpur. *(mai̐ Kānpur me̐ rahatā hū̐) M*∘ میں کانپور میں رہتا ہوں *F*∘ میں کانپور میں رہتی ہوں**

Request them to say it again Modal adverb.: *fir se*, Imperative: *kahiye*

* Please say it again! *barahe meharbānī fir se kahiye.* बराहे मेहरबानी, फिर से कहिये راہ مہربانی پھر سے کہیئے

* I am a new Urdu learner! *maĩ nayā urdū sīkhne wālā hũ.* میں نیا اردو سیکھنے والا ہوں

maĩ nayī urdū sīkhne wālī hũ. میں نئی اردو سیکھنے والی ہوں

* Please speak slowly. (*barahe meharbanī dĥire bolo*) راہ مہربانی دھیرے بولو

* What does it (the word) mean? *is kā matlab?* اس کا کیا مطلب؟

Asking, "what time is it" Adv.: *ab;* Cardinal numerals: 1-12; Phrase: O Clock = *baje*

* What time is it now? *ab kitne baje haĩ?* اب کتنے بجے ہیں؟

Telling time Expressions: quarter past, half past and quarter to

* It is half-past-seven now. *ab sadhe sāt baje haĩ.* اب ساڑھے سات بجے ہیں

* It is quarter-past-three now. *ab savā tīn baje haĩ.* اب سوا تین بجے ہیں

* It is quarter to ten now. *ab paune das baje haĩ.* اب پونے دس بجے ہیں

Telling the day of the week Adv.: *aaj*; Pronouns: names of the seven days

* Today it is Saturday. *āj shanichar hai.* آج سنیچر ہے

(B) EXPRESSIONS

13.4 AFFECTION پیار دکھانے والے جملے

* How nice you are (*āp kitne achhe haĩ*) آپ کیسے اچھے ہیں

* I missed you very much (*muzay āp ki bahut yād āyī*) مجھے آپ کی بہت یاد آئی

* I love him/her (*muzay us se pyar hai*) مجھے اس سے پیار ہے

* When will you see (meet) me? (*āp muzay kab milenge?*) آپ مجھے کب ملیں گے؟

13.5 AFFRMATIVE یقینی جملے

* Yes she will be there (*hã vah vahã hogī*) ہاں وہ وہاں ہوگی

* They will come tomorow (*vah kal āyenge*) وہ کل آئیں گے

* I will give you money (*maĩ āp ko paise dũngā*) میں آپ کو پیسے دونگا

* He did the work (*us ne kām kiyā*) اس نے کام کیا

* Yes, certainly! (*jī, jarūr*) جی، ضرور

13.6 ANGER गुस्सा Gussa غصہ والے جملے

* Don't show me your face again! (*muzay apnī sūrat fir mat dikhanā*) مجھے اپنی صورت پھر مت دکھانا
* Go kill yourself! (Shame on you) (*jāo chullū bhar pāni mẽ ḍūb maro*) جاو چلو بھر پانی میں ڈوب مرو
* What a stupid person you are! (*tum baḍe bevakūf ho*) تم بڑے بیوقوف ہو
* Shut up! (Enough!) (*bas karo, chup karo*) !بس کرو! چپ کرو
* I don't want to listen it (*maĩ kuchh nahĩ sunnā chahtā*) میں کچھ نہیں سننا چاہتا

13.7 ANNOYANCE नाराज़गी Narazgi ناراضگی

* You bother me too much. (*tum muzay bahut sataatae ho*) تم مجھے بہت ستاتے ہو
* They are not honest people. (*vah log īmāndār nahĩ haĩ*) وہ لوگ ایماندار نہیں ہیں
* I can't believe it (*maĩ yakīn nahĩ kr saktā*) میں یقین نہیں کر سکتا
* Why he contradicts me? (*vah merī bāt kyõ kāṭa-tā hai?*) وہ میری بات کیوں کاٹتا ہے؟
* Why do you waste your time? (*tum kyõ vaqt jāyā karte ho?*) تم کیوں وقت ضائع کرتے ہو؟
* She is mad with me (*vah mujh par naraz hai*) وہ مجھ سے ناراض ہے
* Who can I trust! (*maĩ kis par yakīn karũ*) ! میں کس پر یقین کروں
* I hate it. (*muzay is se nafrat hai*) مجھے اس سے نفرت ہے
* He is a nuisance! (*us ne nāk mẽ dam kar rakhā hai*) اس نے ناک میں دم کر رکھا ہے
* She cheated me (*us ne muzay dhokhā diyā*) اسنے مجھے دھوکھا دیا
* He is a fool (*kvah gadhā hai*) وہ گدھا ہے

13.8 APOLOGY معافی، درخواست والے جملے

* Please excuse me (*muzay māf kījiye*) مجھے معاف کیجیئے
* Please don't mind it (*meharbānī kar ke āp is kā burā na mānẽ*) مہربانی کر کے آپ اس کا برا نہ مانیں
* I am sorry! (*maĩ dukhī hũ, maĩ sharmindā hũ*) میں شرمندہ ہوں , میں دکھی ہوں
* I am sorry! (*muzay afsos hai*) مجھے افسوس ہے
* It's my mistake (*yah merī galti hai*) یہ میری غلطی ہے

* I beg your pardon (maĩ āp se māfī chāhtā hũ) میں آپ سے معافی چاہتا ہوں
* Excuse my pronunciation (mere galat lafaz māf karẽ) میرے غلط لفظ معاف کریئے
* My apologies (māf kījiye) معاف کیجئے
* That's alright (koī harj nahĩ, koi bāt nahĩ, ṭhīk hai) ٹھیک ہے , کوئی حرج نہیں , کوئی بات نہیں

13.9 CONSENT रज़ामंदी Razamandi رضامندی والے جملے

* As you wish, Sir! (jaisī āp kī marzī, Sahāb) جیسی آپ کی مرضی صاحب
* That's absolutely correct (yah bilkul ṭhīk hai) یہ بالکل ٹھیک ہے
* You are correct (āp kā kahnā ṭhīk hai) آپ کا کہنا ٹھیک ہے
* I have no objection (muzay koī aitrāz nahĩ) مجھے کوئی اعتراض نہیں
* I agree (maĩ qbūl kartā hũ) میں قبول کرتا ہوں
* Of course (beshak) بےشک
* It's true (yah sach hai) یہ سچ ہے
* I accept(muzay manzūr hai, maĩ manzūr kartā hũ) مجھے منظور ہے میں منظور کرتا ہوں
* I give my consent (maĩ manzurī detā hũ) میں منظوری دیتا ہوں

13.10 CONSOLATION تسلی دینے والے جملے

* How sad, it's very sad (baḍe afsos kī bāt hai) بڑے افسوس کی بات ہے
* It was God's will! (khudā kī yahī marzī thī) خدا کی یہ مرضی تھی
* Have faith (bharosa rakho) بھروسہ رکھو
* The danger will go away (khatra ṭal jāyegā) خطرہ ٹل جائیگا
* My sympathy is with you (merī hamdardī āp ke sāth hai) میری ہمدردی آپ کے ساتھ ہے
* I offer my condolences. (main apnā dukh jāhir krtā hũ) میں اپنا دکھ ظاہر کرتا ہوں

13.11 EMPHATIC جور دینے والے جملے

* Don't forget! (bhūl na jānā) بھول نہ جانا
* Do come tomorrow (kal zarūr ānā) کل ضرور آنا
* Are you happy now? (kyā ab tum khush ho? ab to khush ho na?) کیا اب تم خوش ہو؟ اب توخوش ہو نہ ؟
* At least you are happy (kam se kam tum to khush ho) کم سے کم تم توخوش ہو !

* Indeed we won (*wākaī ham jīte*) واقعی ہم جیتے

* I will love you forever. *maĩ tumhẽ hamesha ke liye pyār karũngā* میں تمہیں ہمیشہ کے لیئے پیار کروں گا

13.12 ENCOURAGEMENT हौसला Hosla حوصلہ

* Rest assured (*yakīn kījiye*) یقین کیجئے
* Stop worrying (*fikr nah karo*) فکر نہ کرو
* Don't worry (*fikr mat karo*) فکر مت کرو
* Don't be afraid (*ḍaro mat*) ڈرو مت
* Don't hesitate (*hichkichānā mat*) ہچکچانہ مت
* Don't be nervous (*ghabrāo mat*) گھبراو مت

13.13 EXCLAMATORY اسمیحا

* My God (*hi rabbā*) ہائے ربا
* What a hard life! (*kitnī muskil hai zindagī*) کتنی مشکل ہے زندگی
* How beautiful (*kitnī khūbsūrat hai*) کتنی خوبصورت ہے
* I wish I was there (*kāsh maĩ vahā̃ hota*) کاش میں وہاں ہوتا

13.14 IMPERATIVE, Order or Request اسمراجی جملے

* Keep quiet (*chup raho*) چپ رہو
* Keep the window open (*khiḍkī khulī rakho*) کھڑکی کھلی رکھو
* Please open the door for me (*meherbānī kar ke mere liye dervāzā kholo*)
مہربانی کر کے میرے لئے دروازہ کھولو
* Drive slowly (*āhistā clāo*) آہستہ چلائو
* Be aware (*is kā khayāl rakho*) اس کا خیال رکھو
* Move aside (*ek taraf ho jāo*) ایک طرف ہوجائو
* Let me see (*muzay dekhne do*) مجھے دیکھنے دو
* Just listen (*suno to, zarā suno*) سنو تو, ذرا سنو

* Come soon! (*jaldī ānā*) جلدی آنا
* Look ahead (*sāmne dekho*) سامنے دیکھو
* Go back (*vāpas jāo*) واپس جاؤ * Go ahead (*āge bad̤ho*) آگے بڑھو

13.15 INTERROGATIVE سوالیہ جملے

* What do you mean? (*āp ka matlab?*) آپ کا مطلب؟
* What does it mean? (*is ka matlab?*) اس کا مطلب؟
* What are you doing? (*āp kyā kar rahe haĩ?*) آپ کیا کر رہے ہیں؟
* Where is Waldo? (*Wāld̤o kahã hai?*) والڈو کہاں ہے؟
*Which train will you take? (*āp kaunsi gād̤ī lenge?*) آپ کونسی گاڑی لینگے
* When is your exam? (*āp ki imtihān kab hai?*) آپ کا امتحان کب ہے؟
* Why are you quiet? (*āp kyõ chup haĩ?*) آپ کیوں چپ ہیں؟
* Who is coming tomorrow? (*kal kaun ā rhā hai?*) کل کون آ رہا ہے؟

13.16 NEGATIVE منفی جملے ; انکار والے جملے

* Why did't you write me? (*āp ne muzay kyõ nahĩ likhā?*) آپ نے مجھے کیوں نہیں لکھا؟
* I don't know (*maĩ nahĩ jāntā*) میں نہیں جانتا
* The letter hasn't come yet (*khat abhī nahĩ āyā*) خط ابھی نہیں آیا
* I will not be with you tomorrow (*kal maĩ āp ke sath nahĩ hūngā*) کل میں آپ کے ساتھ نہیں ہونگا
* Don't go there (*vahã mat jao*) وہاں مت جاؤ

13.17 QUANTITATIVE or NUMERICAL مقررہ جملے

* Do you have any money? (*kyā āp ke pas kuchh pise haĩ?*) آپ کو کچھ پیسے ہیں؟
* Is there anybody? (*vahã koī hai kyā?*) وہاں کوئی ہے کیا؟
* Wait a little bit (*thod̤ā rukiye*) تھوڑا رکیئے
* How much is enough? (*kitnā bas hai?*) کتنا کافی ہے؟
* It is too much (*yah bahut jyādā hai*) یہ بہت زیادہ ہے

* He is absolutely stupid (*vah bilkul pāgal hai*) وہ بالکل پاگل ہے

* It is very nice (*yah bahut achhā hai*) یہ بہت اچھا ہے

* It is not even Half (*yah to ādhā bhī nahī̃ hai*) یہ تو آدھا بھی نہیں ہے

* Give me One-forth (quarter) part (*muzay chauthāī hissā do*) مجھے چوتھائی حصہ دو

* Please take One-third (*tīsarā hissā lo*) تیسرا حصہ لو

* Who took Tow-thirds of this? (*iskā do-tihāī kisne liyā?*) اس کا دو تہائی کس نے لیا

* Leave One-fifth of that (*ua kā pānchwā hissa choḍ do*) اس کا پانچویں حصہ چھوڑ دو

* The price has Doubled (*kīmat dugunī ho gayī*) قیمت دگنی ہو گی

* The price has Trippled (*kīmat tīn guna baḍh gayī*) قیمت تین گنا بڑھ گی

* This is my First time (*yah merī pahli bari hai*) یہ میری پہلی باری ہے

* Is it your Second time? (*yah āp ki dūsarī bāri hai kyā?*) یہ آپ کی دوسری باری ہے کیا؟

* He came Third time (*vah tīsarI bar āyā*) وہ تیسری بار آیا

* Sit on the Fourth chair (*chauthī kursi par baiṭho*) چوتھی کرسی پر بیٹھو

* The Fifth house is mine (*pānchva ghar merā hai*) پانچواں گھر میرا ہے

* Whose is the Sixth car? (*chhaṭhī gāḍī kiskī hai?*) گاڑی کس کی ہے؟ چھٹی

* Where is the Seventh boy? (*sātvā̃ laḍkā khā̃ hai?*) ساتواں لڑکا کہاں ہے؟

* Who is Eighth? (*āṭhvā̃ number kiskā hai?*) آٹھواں نمبر کس کا ہے؟

* The Ninth man died! (*nawā̃ ādmī mar gayā*) نواں آدمی مر گیا

* The Tenth day of the month (*mahīne ka dasvā̃ din*) مہینے کا دسواں دن

13.18 QUARREL جھگڑے والے جملے

* What wrong I have done to you? (*maĩ ne Ap kā kyā bigāḍā hai?*) میں نے آپ کا کیا بگاڑا ہے؟

* Why do you always fight with him? (*tum us se hameshā kyõ laḍte ho?*) تم اس سے ہمیشہ کیوں لڑتے ہو؟

* Don't get excited (*josh mẽ mat āo*) جوش میں مت آؤ * Ok! (*thīk hai*) ٹھیک ہے

* Are you out of your mind? (*tumhāre hosh to ṭhikane haĩ?*) تمہارے ہوش تو ٹھکانے ہیں؟

* Get out of here! (*yahā̃ se haṭ jāo*) یہاں سے ہٹ جاو * Stop it now! (*ab band karo*) اب بند کرو

* Now shake hands (*ab ek dūsare se hāth milāo*) اب ایک دوسرے سے ہاتھ ملاؤ

13.19 CHILDRENS' POEMS

1. A BLIND PERSON

اندھا

اںک اندھا ںصںب کا مارا، جا رہا تھا غریب بیچارا
چلتا ہے ٹیکتا ہوا لاٹھی، دونوں آنکھیں ہیں نور سے خالی

آہٹیں آنے جانے والوں کی، سن کے ہوتی ہے اس کو بیتابی
کیا بتائے کس کو بد قسمت، غم سے ہوتی ہے دل کی جو حالت

یہ درختوں کے پھول اور پتے باغ کے یہ ہرے بھرے پودے
چاندنی، دھوپ، روشنی، سایہ آج تک کبھی نظر نہیں آیا

تم کو اندھا اگر ملے کوئی، پیار سے تم مدد کرو اس کی
راستہ ٹھیک اس کو بتلا دو، یا جہاں جانا چاہے پہنچا دو

2. THE WATERMILL

پن چکی

نہر پر چل رہی ہے پن چکی، دھن کی پوری ہے کام کی پکی
بیٹھی یہ نہیں کبھی تھک کر، اس کے پیسے کو ہے سدا چکر
بھر کے لاتی ہے گاریوں میں اناج، شہر کے شہر اس کے ہیں محتاج
پانی رستا ہو یا چلے آندھی، اس نے چلنے کی شرط ہے باندھی
علم سیکھو پڑھو سبق یکسوں، اور آگے بڑھے چلو یکسوں

LESSON 14

URDU LITERATURE

The notable Urdu literary activity begins with the Sūfī mystic musician Ab'ul Hasan Yamīn al-Dīn Khusrau (1253-1325) ابوالحسن یمین الدین خسرو better known as Amīr Khusrow Dehlawī امیر خسرو دہلوی Born at Badaun, he flourished during the reign of Sultan Ghias-ud-dīn Balban (r. 1266-1287). Following Khusrau's Urdu *Diwān, Ghazal, Masnavi, Qata, Qqwwālī, Rubai, Do-Beti* and *Tarkibhand* writings, the next Urdu literary milestone is the *Dohā* compositions of Sant Kabir (1440-1518). Then the chronology of the Urdy poetry contunues through our great Muslim as well as Hindu forefathers manely, Muhammad Quli Qutub Shah (1565-1611), Wali Muhammad Wali, Deccani (1667-1707), Mirza Mazhar Jan-e-Janaan (1699-1781), Mirza Mohammed Rafi Sauda (1713-1781), Khwaja Mir Dard, (1721-1785), Mir Taqi Mir (1722-1808), Nazeer Akbarabadi, (1740-1830), Daya Shankar Kaul Nasim, (1811-1845), Khwaja Haidar Ali Atish, (1778-1846), Hakim Momin Khan Momin, (1801-1852), Muhammad Ibrahim Khan, Zauq (1789-1854), Bahadur Shah Zafar (1775-1862), Mufti Sadr-Uddin Azurda (1788-1869), Mirza Ghalib (1797-1869), Mir Babbar Ali Anis (1803-1874), Mirza Salaamat Ali Dabeer (1803-1875), Wajid Ali Shah Akhtar (1827-1887), Amir Meenai (1826-1900), Nawab Mirza Khan Dagh Dehlawi, (1831-1905), Durga Sahay Saroor (1873-1910), Bekhud Badayuni (1857-1912), Altaf Hussain (1837-1914), Khwaja Altaf Hussain Hali (1837-1914), Shibli Nomani (1857-1914), Maulana Shibli Numani (1857-1914), Akbar Allahabadi (1846-1921), Brij Narayan Chakbast (1882-1926), Ram Parshad Bismil (1867-1927), Ashfaq Allah Khan (1900-1927), Muhammed Ali Jauhar (1878-1931), Munshi Premchand (1880-1936), Muhammed Iqbal (1873-1938), Akhtar Sheerani (1905-1948), Hasrat Mohani (1875-1951), Syed Ghulam Bhik Nairang (1875-1952), Asrar-Ul-Haq Majaz (1911-1955), Maulana Zafar Ali Khan (1873-1956), Jigar Muradabadi, (1890-1960), Tilok Chand Mehroom (1885-1966), Shakeb Jalali (1932-1966), Makhdoom Mahiuddin (1908-1969), Shakeel Badayuni (1916-1970), Mustafa Zaidi (1930-1970), Nasir

Kazmi, (1925-1972), Ravish Siddiqui (1909-1971), Majeed Amjad (1914-1974), Noon Meem Rashid (1910-1975), Jan Nisar Akhtar (1914-1976), Krishan Chander (1914-1977), Saeeda Urooj Mazhar, (1916-1978), Ibn-e-Insha, (1927-1978), Sahir Ludhianvi, (1921-1980), Nushoor Wahidi (1911-1981), Firaq Gorakhpuri, Raghupati Sahay (1896-1982), Shabir Hasan Josh Malihabadi (1898-1982), Hafeez Jullundhry (1900-1982), Saghir Nizami (1905-1982), Ihsan Danish (1914-1982), Josh Malihabadi, (1898-1982), Faiz Ahmed Faiz (1911-1984), Ayyub Sabir (1923-1989), Yazdani Jalandhari (1915-1990), Gopal Mittal (1906-1993), Habib Jalib (1928-1993), Waheed Akhtar (1934-1996), Obaidullah Aleem (1939-1997), Dilawar Figar (1928-1998), Zamir Jafri, Zamir (1916-1999), Khumar Barabankvi, (1919-1999), Iqbal Ahmed Suhel (1921-1999), Hasrat Jaipuri (1922-1999), Syed Al-e-Ahmad (1932-1999), Ali Sardar Jafri (1913-2000), Majrooh Sultanpuri (1919-2000), Qateel Shifai, (1919-2001), Kaifi Azmi (1915-2002), Jon Elia (1931-2003), Jagannath Azad (1918-2004), Shan-ul-Haq Haqqee (1917-2005), Ahmed Nadeem Qasmi, (1916-2006), Munir Niazi (1928-2006), Ahmad Faraz (1931-2008), Shabnam Romani, (1928-2009), ...etc. A few of the samples and examples of their writings are :

MUHAMMAD IQBAL

محمد اقبال

Tarānā

ہندی ترانہ

سارے جہاں سے اچھا ہندوستاں ہمارا

ہم بلبلیں ہیں اس کی وہ گلستاں ہمارا

پربت وہ سب سے اونچا ہمسایہ آسماں کا

وہ سنتری ہمارا وہ پاسباں ہمارا

مذہب نہیں سکھاتا آپس میں بیر رکھنا

ہىدى ہيں ہم وطن ہے ہىدوستاں ہمارا
یوماں مصرروماسب مٹ گئے جہاں سے
اں مک مگر ہے ماقی مام وساں ہمارا
کحھ مات ہے کہ ہستی مسی نہیں ہماری
صدیوں رہا ہے دشمن دورے جہاں ہمارا
اقبال کوئی محرم اپنا نہیں جہاں میں
معلوم کیا کسی کو دردے سہاں ہمارا

खारे जहाँ से अच्छा हिंदूस्ताँ हमारा। *sāre jahā̐ se achhā̐ hindustā̐ hmārā,*
हम बुलबुलें हैं उसकी वो गुलसिताँ हमारा।। *hum bulbulē̐ haĩ qsa kī vo gulsitā̐ hamārā.*

पर्बत वो सब से ऊँचा हमसाया आसमाँ का। *parbat ho sab se ū̐nchā hamasāyā āsmā̐ kā,*
वो संतरी हमारा वो पासवाँ हमारा।। *vo santarī hamārā vo pāsawā̐ hamārā.*

मजहब नहीं सिखाता आपस में बैर रखना। *majhab nahī̐ sikhātā āpasa mē̐ bair rakhanā,*
हिंदी हैं हम वतन है हिंदूस्ताँ हमारा।। *hindī haĩ hum vatan hai hindūstā̐ hamārā.*

यूनान मिस्त्र रोमाँ सब मिट गये जहाँ से। *yūnāna misrromā sab miṭ gaye jahā̐ se,*
अब तक मगर है बाक़ी नाम-औ-निशाँ हमारा।। *ab tak magar hai bāqi nām-o-nishā̐ hamārā.*

कुछ बात है कि हस्ति मिटती नहीं हमारी। *kuchh bāt hai ki hasti miṭatī nahī̐ hamārī,*
सदियों रहा है दुश्मन दौर-ए-जहाँ हमारा।। *sadiyō̐ rahā hai dushman daur-e-jahā̐ hamārā.*

इक़बाल कोई मरहुम अपना नहीं जहाँ में। *iqbāl koī marhūm apanā nahī̐ jahā̐ mē̐*
मालूम क्या किसी को दर्द-ए-निहाँ हमारा।। *mālūm kuā kisī ko dard-e-nihā̐ hamārā.*

SANT KABIR

سنت کبیر

Dohā

دوہا

چلتی چکی دیکھ کے پڑا کبیرا روئے
دو پاٹن کے بیچ میں ژابت بچا نہ کوئے

1

برا جو دیکھن میں چلا بئرا نہ ملیا کوئے
جو من اپنا کھوجیا مجھ سے برا نہ کوئے

2

کل کرے سو آج کر آج کرے سو اب
پل میں پرلے ہوت ہے باد کروگے کب

3

بڑا ہوا تو یہں ہوا جیسا پیڑ کھجور
پنتھی کو چھایا پھل لاگت اتی دور

4

کبیر کھڑا بازار میں مانگے سب کی خیر
نہ کاہو سے دوستی نہ کاہو سے بیر

5

AMIR KHUSRAU

امر خسرو

nazm

نظم

نمی دانم چہ منزل بود شب جائے کہ من بودم
بہ ہرسو رقص بسمل بود شب جائے کہ من بودم
پری پیکر نگارے سروقدے لالہ رخسارے
سراپا آفت دل بود شب جائے کہ من بودم
خداخود میر مجلس بود اندر لامکاں خسرو
محمد شمع محفل بود شب جائیکہ من بودم

MIRZA GALIB

مرزا غالب

Ghazal

غزل

مگر لکھوائے کوئی اس کا خط تو ہم سے لکھوائے
ہوئی صبح اور گھر سے ، کان پر رکھ کر قلم ، نکلے

ڈرے کیوں میرا قاتل ، کیا رہے گا اس کی گردن پر
وہ خون ، جو چشم تر سے عمر بھر یوں دم بہ دم نکلے

ہوئی جن سے توقع خستگی کی داد پانے کی
وہ ہم سے بھی زیادہ خستہ تیغ ستم نکلے

محبت میں نہیں ہے فرق جینے اور مرنے کا
اسی کو دیکھ کر جیتے ہیں جس کافر پہ دم نکلے

بھرم کھل جائے ظالم تیرے قامت کی درازی کا
اگر اس طرہ پر پیچ و خم کا پیچ و خم نکلے

BAHADUR SHAH ZAFAR

بہادر ساہ ظفر

Bahadur Shah Zafar was the last Mughal emperor to rule India. After the revolt of 1857 also called the First war of Indian Independence, he was arrested and exiled to Rangoon. He was a great lover of poetry.

Ghazal

عرل

لگتا نہیں ہے دل میرا اجڑے دیار میں
کس کی بنی ہے عالمے ناپائے دار میں

که دوان حسرتوں سے کهیں اور جا بسیں
اتنی جگه کہاں ہے دلے داغدار میں

عمر دراز مانگ کے لائے تھے چار دن
دو آرزو میں کٹ گئے دو انتظار میں

کتنا بدنصیب ظفر دفن کے لیئے
دو گز زمین بھی نه ملی کوئے یار میں

Lagtaa nahin hai dil meraa ujday dayaar mein
kis ki bani hai aalam-e-naa_paayedaar mein

kah do in hasraton se kahin aur jaa basein
itani jagah kahaan hai dil-e-daagdaar mein

umr-e-daraaz maang kar laaye they chaar din
do arzoo mein kat gaye do intezaar mein

kitnaa hai bad_naseeb "Zafar" dafn key liye
do gaz zamin bhi na mili kuu-e-yaar mein

KAIFI AZMI

کیفی اعظمی

Nazm

نظم

حریت کو آج پھر ہے ابن حیدرؑ کی تلاش
وقت کو پھر ہے کروڑوں میں بہتر کی تلاش
زندگی کو پھر ہے اک جاں باز رہبر کی تلاش
پھر جوانی کھوتے کو ہے وہ نشانِ حریت
پھر ہوئی ہے دوش عباسؑ دلاور کی تلاش
پھر حمیت اٹھی ہے پھر ہے عزت گرم کار
پھر ہوئی ہے زندگی کو جوش اکبرؑ کی تلاش
دیکھنا کیفی نشانِ حریت لہرائے گا
جب جہاں کو عزم شیر کربلا مل جائے گا

JAN NISAR AKHTAR

جاں نثار اختر

Sher

شیر

اشار میرے ہوں تو زمانے کے لیئے ہیں
کچھ شیر فقط ان کو سنانے کے لیئے ہیں

ashaar mere yuun to zamaane ke liye hain kuchh sher faqat unako sunaane ke liye hain

SHAKIL BADAUNI

شکیل بدایونی

Gānā: From the Hindi Movie, Sitara

گانا

تقدیر کی گردش کیا کم تھی اس پر یہ قیامت کر بیٹھے
بیتابی دل جب حد سے بڑھی گھبرا کے محبت کر بیٹھے

آنکھوں میں چھلکتے ہیں آنسو دل چھپکے چھپکے روتا ہے
وہ بات ہمارے بس کی نہ تھی جس بات کی محبت کر بیٹھے

غم ہم نے خوشی سے مول لیا اس پر بھی ہوئی یہ نادانی
جب دل کی امیدیں ٹوٹ گیئں قسمت سے شکایت کر بیٹھے